Keep the Rest of the Class Reading & Writing . . .

While You Teach Small Groups

60 High-Interest Reproducible Activities—Perfect for Learning Centers—
That Build Comprehension, Vocabulary, and Writing Skills

BY SUSAN FINNEY

SCHOLASTIC
PROFESSIONAL BOOKS

New York • Toronto • London • Auckland • Sydney
Mexico City • New Delhi • Hong Kong

Cover design by Pamela Simmons
Interior design by Grafica, Inc.

ISBN 0-590-68566-X
Copyright © 2000 by Susan Finney, all rights reserved.
Printed in USA

Table of Contents

Table of Contents

Introduction

As you cycle children in and out of

guided reading groups, facilitate

a variety of literacy activities, or

assist individual students, what

are the other children doing?

The key to maintaining high-quality uninterrupted instructional time is a classroom management strategy that supports students working independently. The solution for me, and for the teachers with whom I've shared these ideas, is to maintain a literacy focus by keeping all students reading and writing.

I have found three components for creating "win-win" classroom management, where expectations are clearly stated, everyone's learning, everyone's productive, and you can teach.

1. Establish literacy centers

If you're shaking your head in wonderment at the idea of returning to the use of centers, consider education's proverbial pendulum swings. It has been said that an experienced teacher has probably been bonked on the head at least three times by that pendulum. Centers were an integral part of the classroom environment for many years and, in this case, there's good reason for the pendulum's return—the purpose of centers has been redefined. Designed to supplement direct instruction, their focus is on literacy skill-building and content-area study skills. Since the research emphatically states that teacher-directed small groups that allow children to actively participate is essential for improving reading instruction, the other children need a place to go—a structured place.

The use of literacy centers supports a balanced reading program. Centers allow for self-directed learning, and—because many centers offer options and choices—they are easily adapted to different ability levels. Flexible grouping is more readily accomplished when students in temporary groups can move smoothly to centers in a rotation. Literacy centers also provide an opportunity for independent reading, word study, vocabulary building, investigation of different genres and literary devices, and collaboration. The center ideas included in this book have been tested, adapted, reviewed, and refined so that you will be able to add them easily to your classroom repertoire and successfully put them into practice.

2. Initiate a variety of literacy-focused activities for small groups

Literacy centers are, by definition, places where literacy-focused activities take place. There are, however, wonderful literacy-focused activities which are ideal for heterogeneous small groups yet are not strictly center oriented. Rather than going to a designated place to work, small groups of children may collaborate on special projects which may be incorporated into the center rotation or assigned. Numerous examples are mentioned in the book. The focus remains the same (whether it's a literacy center or a small-group literacy-focused activity), structure is provided, routines are established, and meaningful literacy learning is taking place.

3. Implement long-term, ongoing projects

Ongoing, long-term projects logically complement the use of literacy centers; simply put, they are literacy-focused activities on a large scale. When your students say, "I've finished, what do I do now?" you have answers: "Work on your Newbery Book Reports," or "Work on your Caldecott Book Project," or "Work on your Dewey Decimal Bingo Project." You get the idea. Something is always going on.

Literacy centers, literacy-focused activities, and ongoing projects reinforce literacy learning, refine skills, and strategically maintain goal-oriented academic work. It is wise to remember, as a mentor of mine once remarked: "Keeping kids busy, happy, and good does not ensure learning." With literacy as the focus, these activities not only ensure learning, they are truly the ultimate classroom management strategy.

Susan Finney

Literacy Centers and Logistics
Managing Your Classroom, Keeping Your Sanity

Over the past few years, I've discovered that the most workable classroom management plans emerge when teachers collaboratively focus on solutions. One idea piggybacks on another, and the original strategy branches out to become a number of strategies, each a variation to suit specific classroom needs.

This chapter is a tribute to some of the most creative people I know—teachers whose lives are so busy that they don't have time for more work. The entrepreneurial spirit lives in the classroom, thank goodness, and the ideas that follow reflect unique adaptations of a management system for making literacy centers easy to implement.

Some thoughts about literacy centers:

➤➤ Literacy centers provide the structure for managing students while you teach small, needs-based groups.

➤➤ Literacy centers allow students to work independently and collaboratively as they practice literacy skills.

➤➤ Literacy centers are designed to complement learning objectives with opportunities for both challenge and enrichment.

➤ Literacy-focused activities can be combined with literacy centers.

➤ To ensure that there is always something to "do" for students who are not working at centers, or for students who have completed center work, there should be an ongoing activity—something "big" that continues over an extended period of time.

Some thoughts on grouping:

➤ Homogeneous small groups should meet for guided reading instruction in texts based on ability level. These small groups should be balanced with flexible, multiability grouping—for instance, literature circles—to avoid the stigma of static groups.

➤ Literacy centers and literacy-focused activities provide the opportunity for heterogeneous, multiability groups.

➤ Heterogeneous small groups can work together at literacy centers, on literacy-focused activities, and on long-term projects.

➤ Grouping formats may include dyads, triads, groups of four, groups of seven to ten, half the class, the whole class, random grouping, and task or activity grouping.

Some thoughts on the physical environment:

➤ It doesn't take a tabletop to make a center. Centers can be folders stapled to the wall or tacked to a bulletin board with activity sheets inside. A center can be the top of a bookshelf, the seat of a chair, a cabinet or a closet door. Centers can lean against the wall or be hung from the ceiling. Centers can be centers in name only. Do what you can with what you have.

➤ Think about how many centers you will need to provide rotation options for your students. There are some centers that will accommodate three or four students at a time, some centers that don't restrict numbers because they are simply repositories for the activity pages, and some centers designed just for two students. Remember too that the ongoing, long-term project will absorb several students.

Understanding your options for adding, changing, or rotating centers:

➤ When centers are introduced, whether it's the beginning or well into the term, it is absolutely essential that time is spent explaining each one. This helps avoid the "I don't understand" interruptions, emphasizes the importance you place on your students correctly completing each of the activities, and provides an opportunity for reiterating standards and the rotation plan. Plan on five to 10 minutes at each center, circulating around the room to each center location with your students, answering questions as they arise.

➤ Many teachers prefer to keep the same centers for a specific time period. A date is set by which all centers must be completed. Children keep all center work in a folder until that date. If a contract is used, it may be affixed to the front of the folder to build student accountability.

➤ There are times when teachers want to add centers. Several intermediate teachers with whom I've worked have added "challenge" centers to the rotation to differentiate instruction for their intellectually gifted students. By labeling those centers as "optional," they are open to all students, but required for others. A center may also be added when specific skills need reinforcing or when the centers are long-term, and some short-term activities are introduced. As long as there is adequate time to complete the assigned work, centers can be added at any time.

▸▸ If you like the idea of having a permanent writing center or a permanent center devoted to picture book activities, the center can be labeled as such, with different tasks assigned on a rotating basis. Over one two-week period, the writing center could focus on responding to prompts; the next two-week period could focus on modeling one's writing on a specific author's style, and so on.

▸▸ The long-term activities in this book were designed to complement literacy centers. This strategy evolved so students would always have "something to do" when their center work was finished. As the due date approaches and students begin finishing their center assignments, it is imperative that there be an ongoing, long-term activity to physically and mentally absorb the students. One rotation variation described below includes the long-term activity. This activity should be introduced at the same time or earlier than centers are. Most of these long-term activities are designed to last one or two months or more, and they are the key to maintaining the equilibrium in a classroom with literacy centers.

Options for building in accountability and responsibility:

• **Write an open-ended contract, which uses numbers for centers instead of naming them**. (See page 12.) The physical location of the center where the work is to be done should be numbered to identi-

fy it (although a physical location isn't always needed). A folder with the center activity inside can simply have the number on the cover. This allows you to periodically change centers without worrying about constantly changing the contract.

• **Checklists require students to note completed activities**. (See page 13.) A blank form with a place for the title of the center and a check-off column can simplify preparation time and be very effective. As you introduce and explain new centers, students write in the center titles. This flexible format, like the one above, allows for the introduction of new centers to the rotation.

▸▸ **Choice menus require students to complete a specific number of activities from a menu of choices**. (See page 14.) This format is also an excellent way to individualize. Some centers can be "required" for specific students. Simply check off the "required" centers prior to handing out the menus, still leaving room for choice. A choice menu is ideal for less able students as well, since the assignment load can be adapted.

▸▸ **A rubric may be used to assess students' center work and provide an overall grade**. With a rubric, however, it is difficult to factor in performance on individual tasks. Another method of assigning a grade for literacy center work during a defined time period may simply be adding the scores for each activity and then averaging them. One fourth grade teacher decided that some tasks needed to be graded individually, but she holistically graded the others. Students appreciated that flexible and conscientious approach.

▸▸ **As important as it is to take the time to explain centers, it may be even more important to take the time to correct them**. This is best done as a whole-class activity. Plan for at least an hour on the morning or afternoon when centers are due. If time is an issue, consider the time you have saved by being more efficient in your teaching. This is truly not a debatable issue: If these activities are not perceived as important to their learning, if value is not given to correcting them, students will not give quality effort, time, or energy to them. Some of the more open-ended activities may be too subjective for students to self-correct; those should be collected and graded by the teacher. Students must be held accountable for all required center work.

Understanding the rotation options:

▸▸ The premise of the rotation is that it allows you to work with a small group without interruption during your reading/language arts block. This block of time varies from school to school and from classroom to classroom. In an ideal world, that time period would be about two hours; that way, with four reading groups, each would cycle through having approximately one-half hour of instructional time. Beginning with that "ideal world" scenario, adjustments obviously have to be made for fewer or additional reading groups and less than a two-hour time block.

▸▸ Grouping options influence the rotation. One grouping option favored by some teachers is called a random grouping. Students are called to their reading group, and the remainder of the class is directed to center activities, the long-term activity, or literacy-focused activities of some type. Students are not assigned as groups to specific areas but are free to work together at an activity of their choice. When the next group is called to read, students simply leave their current activity and join the teacher. Students leaving the reading group may have work to do at their seats related to their lesson before they join the others.

▸▸ Two sixth grade teachers who have teamed successfully for years favor a more structured approach. (With 60 students between them, it's not hard to see why.) Students who are not reading with the teacher are assigned to one of three specific tasks. One is centers, another is the long-term activity, and the third involves choices from a list of "approved" literacy activities. This list includes silent reading, readers' theater practice, poetry memorization, and journal writing, as well as any work related to the skills being taught in the reading group. Students move in half-hour increments from task to task. Each day begins with a different reading group, which influences the schedule of assigned tasks. Fridays often focus on whole-class activities.

▸▸ A third grade teacher I know solved a problem many of us have encountered. Instead of naming or numbering her reading groups, she has grouped her students according to the title of the book they are reading. Instead of saying, "Will Group Two come up?" she says, "Will the *Fantastic Mr. Fox* Group come up?" Because the group names change frequently (as they finish one book and begin another), she feels that she is avoiding some of the stigma associated with static grouping. Additionally, she often uses the same book with different ability groups, focusing on different skills. She also moves her students into and out of groups depending on the skills being taught. Her group rotation is based on the groups' book, and students move from place to place as a group. Along with literacy centers, she has mandated a silent reading time as part of her schedule.

➤➤ Another variation on the structured rotation has also been successful in a number of classrooms. In addition to the requisite reading group, the rotation includes assigned writing tasks. The writing tasks may not be at centers. Students are to work at their seats on their writing for the designated time period. When new skills are taught, students then have a built-in opportunity for sustained and focused practice. Spelling can also be brought into the language arts rotation in this way.

"It is not hard work that turns students away, it is busy work that destroys them."

That piece of advice, given by one of my mentors, establishes a mindset that is pivotal to successfully implementing literacy centers. We don't have classroom time to waste. What students need is direct involvement and interaction with text, authentic activities designed to build literacy skills, specific assignments that are balanced by opportunities for options and choice, and tasks that allow for both collaboration and independent, self-directed work. Accountability builds responsibility. The contract, checklist, and choice menu are provided as examples that can easily be adapted to your needs and to different grade levels. They are crucial to maintaining and managing literacy centers in your classroom.

Centers Contract

Name _____

Contract Due Date _____

# of center	✔ when finished	Center Activity

Name _____ **Date** _____

Centers Checklist

Center Activity	Date Completed

Which center did you enjoy the most? Give three reasons.

At which center did you learn the most? Why?

Keep the Rest of the Class Reading and Writing ... While You Teach Small Groups   Scholastic Professional Books

Choice Menu

Students are more motivated when they are allowed to make choices. The Choice Menu gives students the opportunity to select literacy-related activities and provides the means by which you can individualize learning tasks for students of differing abilities. Your classroom centers provide the actual choices; the Choice Menu presents them in an appealing format. When students are required to take information and analyze, evaluate, or create something original, there is far more challenge. These higher-level thinking activities are options for all students, but you might want to make them mandatory for your gifted or high-achieving students. While you maintain control by requiring specific tasks, remember to still leave room for student self-selection. The sample below can be adjusted and adapted for grades 3–6.

Choose six of the nine activities.

☐ **Plural noun search:** Find at least 15 plural nouns in one of the books at the library center.	☐ **Using the information in the book *Dandelions*, by Eve Bunting, create a map which would show a possible route the family took to Nebraska.**	☐ **Complete the center for *A River Ran Wild***
☐ **Once you have completed the center for *A River Ran Wild*, find information about other instances of environmental pollution and prepare a report. You may work with a friend.**	☐ **Complete the partner center, "In White Tie and Tails."**	☐ **Using the new vocabulary words in the selection "In White Tie and Tails," create a crossword puzzle.**
☐ **Dictionary Skills Center:** List the guide words for each of the words on your spelling list.	☐ **Compare the illustrations in Allen Say's books to the illustrations in William Steig's books. How do they differ? How do they help tell the story? How is color used? Whose illustrations do you prefer?**	☐ **Complete the Allen Say Author Study center.**

Partner Centers

Partner centers are activities based on a single text on which two students work together. The idea evolved because so often we have one copy of a wonderful book and, other than listening to the book as a read-aloud, an entire class can't take advantage of the learning opportunities the book affords. Partner centers support subject-area studies as well as research and study skills, and your students can use newspaper and magazine articles as well as excerpts from encyclopedias.

Students are allowed and encouraged to work together because it is discussion and collaboration that makes this such an effective learning experience. In your classroom rotation, the use of partner centers can complement other centers in order to accommodate the number of children who will be using the centers.

The activity pages that follow are provided as models to help you in designing your own partner centers. Hopefully they will not only be useful as is, but will be effective as templates for designing your own centers. The intent is to spark your own ideas, to provide an "Aha!" experience (as in, "Aha! I can use that idea with another book that I have!").

PAGE 16
▸▸ MUSING AND PERUSING can be used with any wonderful story. The focus is on metacognition and critical thinking. For centers, try the award-winning Caldecott picture books—many offer sophisticated story lines. Use the form as a book report.

PAGE 17
▸▸ PARTNER READING: FOCUSING ON CHARACTERS helps develop an understanding of characterization and how the characters influence action.

PAGE 19
▸▸ LIBRARY LIL requires students to return to a text for factual information as well as for skill reinforcement. Use the ideas here to create similar pages based on other books.

PAGE 20
▸▸ "IN WHITE TIE AND TAILS" shows how a *Ranger Rick* or *ZooNooz*-type of magazine article can be used to focus on vocabulary building. Note how the strategy of providing the definitions in question format builds in both interest and accountability.

PAGE 21
▸▸ A RIVER RAN WILD demonstrates the use of the cloze technique to prompt students and energize comprehension skills. This story portrays the environmental history of a polluted river.

PAGE 22
▸▸ DANDELIONS is historical fiction in picture book format. The menu format allows for choice—a great motivator. Ideal for studies of the Westward Movement. Fabulous artwork.

PAGE 23
▸▸ "VENUS" focuses on content information using a prereading format known as an anticipation guide. Statements require students to make choices. Note the "I'm not sure" option, which emphasizes that students should pay more attention to text. Students read text after filling in the anticipation guide and then must either "agree" or "disagree" when the "I'm not sure" choice is no longer an option. Consider using this format when introducing new units of study.

PAGE 26
▸▸ A THOUSAND WORDS: LEARNING FROM PHOTOGRAPHS and FINDING INFORMATION IN A PHOTOGRAPH provide center ideas for building visual literacy.

Musing and Perusing

Title: _____

Author: _____

Look at the phrases below. As you read one of the books at this center, think about the phrases. Turn the phrases into sentences that show what you were thinking while you read or after you finished reading.

1. I wonder why _____

_____

2. I don't see how _____

_____

3. I can't believe _____

_____

4. Why did _____

_____

5. It bothered me when _____

_____

6. I was surprised _____

_____

7. I can't really understand _____

_____

8. I began to think of _____

_____

_____

9. When I finished reading, I thought _____

_____

_____

Keep the Rest of the Class Reading and Writing ... While You Teach Small Groups   Scholastic Professional Books

Partner Reading: Focusing on Characters

At this center, you and a partner will read and discuss the same book. Each of you will complete your own worksheet. You may use one of the books at this center or another that you have both read.

Your name: _____   **Partner's name:** _____

Book title: _____

Author: _____

1. On the chart below, list the main characters and give two facts about each:

NAME OF CHARACTER	WHO IS THIS CHARACTER? WHY IS HE/SHE IMPORTANT?	

17

2. Explain something that a character in this story learned.

_____

_____

_____

3. How is a character in this story like someone you know?

_____

_____

4. Which character in this story reminds you of a character in another story you have read?   What are their similarities?

_____

_____

_____

5. Whom would you invite to your home?   Why?

_____

_____

6. Prioritize the characters in order of their importance to the story.   Who is the most important?   Who is next, etc.?

_____

_____

_____

Library Lil

by Suzanne Williams

Answer the questions below on another sheet of paper. Staple this sheet to your answers.

1. What is a tall tale?

2. Why is *Library Lil* a tall tale?

3. Find and write down three examples of hyperbole.

4. Find and write down ten contractions.

5. Lil thought poison ivy, mosquitoes, and what else belonged in the same category? What do you think?

6. When the power lines blew down, the author used another simile to describe what happened to the televisions. What was the simile?

7. Bill didn't believe Lil could move their motorcycles. What did he say he would do if she did?

8. What book did the guys fight over? Who's the author of that book?

9. Write three sentences about Lil's new assistant.

Suzanne Williams, the author of *Library Lil*, decided to write a tall tale about a librarian because kids today know more about librarians than they do about cowboys or lumberjacks. She also made her hero- ine's name alliterative. List five alliterative names you would use for your characters if you were going to write a tall tale.

_____

_____

_____

_____

_____

_____

_____

In White Tie and Tails

Directions: As you read this with your partner, use a highlighter to mark words you do not know. Look up their definitions so you can answer the questions below.

What's black and white and red all over? A sunburned penguin is a definite possibility. What wears a tuxedo each time it goes out to eat? A penguin, of course! Last one. Why did the penguin cross the iceberg? That's obvious. To go with the floe!

Penguins are fascinating birds, but they are birds that do not fly. These flightless denizens are found only in the Southern Hemisphere and range in size from the 41 cm (about 16 inches) blue penguin to the majestic 120+ cm (48 inches) emperor penguin. Of the 17 species of penguins, only three live in Antarctica: the chinstrap, the Adélie, and the emperor.

Because their short legs are far back on their bodies, penguins possess an upright posture that is almost man-like. Over the ages, their wings have become flippered appendages, which serve them well in swimming and diving. Penguins' entire bodies, in fact, are wonderful examples of nature's ability to adapt to any environment. Penguins' bones are solid and help provide extra weight in deep dives down as far as 850 feet (approximately 250 meters). A heavy layer of subcutaneous fat gives heat-saving insulation to a trunk covered with thick down. Small, hard feathers overlap the down, almost like roof shingles, to form a protective covering over all.

The male and female of most species take turns incubating a clutch or one or two eggs on a bare rock, a nest of stones, or, in the case of the emperor, on the male's feet under a fold of abdominal skin. The chicks are fed regurgitated food from their parents until they shed their down and acquire their first full plumage.

Incredibly graceful swimmers, penguins spend much of their time in the water feeding. Porpoising, leaps into the air or onto the land or ice from the water, can catapult a penguin as high as two meters in the air. Leopard seals, which are ferocious and deadly predators of penguins, often prove to be fatal swimming companions when a penguin's jump to safety fails.

1. Which word means leaping into the air or onto the land or ice from the water?

2. Which word means a bird's feathers?

3. Which word means an inhabitant of a particular place?

4. Which word means an external organ or part?

5. Which word means fierce, savage, or violently cruel?

6. Which word means beneath the skin?

7. Which word means to bring partly digested food back from the stomach to the mouth?

8. Which word means resulting in death?

9. Which word means someone who lives by capturing and feeding upon other animals?

10. Which word refers to someone who associates with someone else?

11. Which word means a single piece of floating sea ice?

To the teacher: Fold this section under before duplicating. Answers: 1) porpoising, 2) plumage, 3) denizen, 4) appendage, 5) ferocious, 6) subcutaneous, 7) regurgitated, 8) fatal, 9) predator, 10) companion, 11) floe

A River Ran Wild
An Environmental History

by Lynne Cherry

This is a true story about the Nashua River in Massachusetts. It is a story of how a clean, sparkling river became ecologically dead and how it was restored. Finish the phrases below by choosing important facts to summarize this story.

Almost 600 years ago, _____

_____.

The chief of the native people _____

_____.

The river was important to them because _____

_____.

One day, a trader came and _____

_____.

Settlers came to live by the trading post and _____

_____.

The settlers used the land and the river differently than the Indians had. The settlers changed the lives of

the Indians by _____

_____.

There was a war, and the Indians were driven from the land. Factories were built. Waste was dumped

into the Nashua River. "Progress" created pollution. Oweana and Marion decided to change things.

On a separate piece of paper, explain how this polluted river was cleaned up.

Dandelions

by Eve Bunting

The menu below offers you nine choices. After carefully reading this book with your partner, you may choose any six of the activities to complete. You and your partner do not have to choose the same activities, but discussing your thoughts may give you some good ideas. Please circle the numbers of each of the activities you choose and use that number when you write your answers. All answers are to be in complete sentences. Attach your answer sheet to this page.

1. This picture book is considered historical fiction. What is history? What is fiction? Why is this historical fiction?

2. Sketch a simple map showing the location of Illinois and Nebraska. Find out how far it is from Illinois to Nebraska. If the family traveled about 12 miles a day, how long would it take to reach Nebraska?

3. Describe the members of this family. Tell one or two facts about each one and also how each is important to the story.

4. Illustrators help authors tell their stories. Greg Shed, the illustrator of this book, traveled to Nebraska so that he could see the prairie grasslands. In your opinion, which illustration best helps the author? Describe the illustration and explain how it helps tell the story.

5. Why did settlers in Nebraska have soddie houses? Describe a soddie house.

6. What was this story mostly about? What other stories that you've read remind you of this one?

7. Describe the Svenson family. How were they important to Zoe's family?

8. Do you think *Dandelions* is a good title for this book? Give five reasons.

9. What does the author, Eve Bunting, want us to be thinking about when we've finished reading this book?

Venus (page one)

Name _____ **Date** _____

Read and respond to each statement below **before** you read the information on Venus. Put a check in the "Agree" column if you agree. Put a check in the "Disagree" column if you disagree. If you are not sure, put a check in the "I'm Not Sure" column.

This is the first page of a two-page assignment for the attached article on Venus.

Agree	Disagree	I'm Not Sure	Facts About Venus?
			Venus is the second planet from the sun.
			It is sometimes called Earth's "sister planet."
			Venus spins backward on its axis.
			The surface temperature of Venus is similar to Earth's.
			The "greenhouse effect" on Venus is caused by sulfuric acid.
			A probe landing on Venus would burn up in an hour.
			There are no mountains on Venus.
			Venus has a valley similar to the Grand Canyon.
			A day on Venus is equal to 158 Earth days.
			Venus has 17 moons.
			There are constant thunderstorms and lightning.
			Venus is completely encircled by clouds.
			The gravity on Venus is about the same as gravity on Earth.
			Venus has no moons, but sunrise and sunset are just like sunrise and sunset on Earth.
			Astronomers have depended on radar to learn about Venus.

Venus (page two)

Name _____ **Date** _____

Now, carefully read the fact sheet on Venus and either "Agree" or "Disagree" with the information presented. Put a check in the "Agree" column if you agree. Put a check in the "Disagree" column if you disagree.

Agree	Disagree	Facts About Venus?
		Venus is the second planet from the sun.
		It is sometimes called Earth's "sister planet."
		Venus spins backward on its axis.
		The surface temperature of Venus is similar to Earth's.
		The "greenhouse effect" on Venus is caused by sulfuric acid.
		A probe landing on Venus would burn up in an hour.
		There are no mountains on Venus.
		Venus has a valley similar to the Grand Canyon.
		A day on Venus is equal to 158 Earth days.
		Venus has 17 moons.
		There are constant thunderstorms and lightning.
		Venus is completely encircled by clouds.
		The gravity on Venus is about the same as gravity on Earth.
		Venus has no moons, but sunrise and sunset are just like sunrise and sunset on Earth.
		Astronomers have depended on radar to learn about Venus.

Venus

Venus, the second planet from the Sun, is the hottest world in the solar system. It is blanketed by a thick layer of clouds that heat its surface like a greenhouse garden. But with a surface temperature of almost 900 degrees Fahrenheit (480°C), this place is no garden!

Other than its temperature, Venus is so similar to Earth that it is sometimes called Earth's "sister planet." Its diameter and mass are almost identical to Earth's. Why, then, is it so hot?

The "greenhouse effect" on Venus is caused by its atmosphere. Energy from the Sun can get through the atmosphere to the planet's surface, but it cannot escape again into space. The trapped heat builds up, making the planet grow hotter and hotter. The same thing happens in an automobile on a hot day. Sunlight comes through the windows and warms the inside of the car, but the heat is trapped. The inside of a car can get dangerously hot in just a few minutes. And Venus has been heating up for billions of years.

Even though Venus' orbit brings it closer to Earth than any other planet, its blanket of clouds kept much of Venus a mystery. But space probes sent by the Soviet Union and the United States, as well as studies with ground-based radar, have allowed astronomers to "see" the surface of Venus for the first time. The first exploration of Venus by radar was in 1962. It revealed that Venus spins backward on its axis. The length of a day on Venus is equal to 243 Earth days. If you could see the Sun through Venus' cloud cover, it would rise in the west and set in the east. Venus has no known moons.

Space probes have revealed that the atmospheric pressure at the surface of Venus is 90 times that of Earth's—four times higher than the highest pressure ever endured by humans. This atmosphere consists mainly of carbon dioxide—the same gas that puts the fizz in soft drinks. It is not breathable. In addition, the clouds of Venus produce drops of sulfuric acid, a poisonous chemical.

Daytime on Venus is about as bright as a cloudy day on Earth, and the winds on the ground are gentle. The ground on Venus is flat and lifeless, as you would expect from the great weight of the planet's atmosphere. Gravel and flattened boulders are scattered over the plains. Because of the heat and pressure on Venus, no probe landing there has ever survived for more than an hour.

More recent radar observations by the Magellan spacecraft have allowed scientists to map almost the entire surface of the planet. Magellan discovered mountains on Venus that are higher than any on Earth, as well as a valley that is longer and deeper than the Grand Canyon. It also revealed that the surface of Venus may contain active volcanoes, which occasionally spew great geysers of molten rock and hot gas into the already steamy atmosphere.

If You Went to Venus

Because of Venus' heavy atmosphere, the planet's air pressure is very high. Air pressure is defined as the weight of the air in the atmosphere pressing down on you. On Earth, we don't notice the air pressure at all. The thick atmosphere on Venus would make it very difficult to see objects very far away from you.

Since carbon dioxide is poisonous to humans, you would not be able to breathe on Venus. Thick, high clouds would make the Sun just a yellow-orange smear of light.

Although the gravity on Venus is about the same as on Earth, the weight of the atmosphere would crush you.

There are always thunderstorms somewhere on the planet, and lightning flashes about 25 times every second.

Although there are mountains and valleys on Venus, most of the planet is fairly flat, with very low hills. There is some dust and gravel, but no soil—only flat, broken rocks.

Excerpted from:
StarDate Guide to the Solar System,
The University of Texas at Austin.
McDonald Observatory.
Used with permission.
(512) 471-5285.
http://stardate.utexas.edu

A Thousand Words:
Learning From Photographs

What can you learn from a picture? Visual literacy will add a different dimension to the center work in your classroom. There are countless books and magazines which use photographs to complement text. Textbooks, magazines, nature-oriented nonfiction, biographies and autobiographies are all vehicles for encouraging students to use information from photographs to build writing skills. Students who are spatial, kinesthetic learners will often "see" more than their linguistic, logical-mathematical peers.

1. Students, working together, are each to have a copy of "Finding Information in a Photograph" (page 27). They will "notice" more if there is discussion. Social studies and science books are excellent sources for interesting photographs.

2. Once the form is filled in, have students use their answers to create one or more paragraphs.

3. Piggyback on this by using photographs as a storyboard to provide a visual prompt for creative storytelling.

As an independent activity, have students create their own photographic essays (a series of captioned pictures which tell a story).

The books below are just a sampling of what may be used:

Margaret Bourke-White: Photographing the World by Eleanor Ayer. (ISBN 0-87518-513-4).

Prairie Visions: The Life and Times of Solomon Butcher by Pam Conrad. (ISBN 0-06-446135-1). Paperback. A photographic history of Nebraska's pioneers.

Eye on the Wild: A Story About Ansel Adams by Julie Dunlap. (ISBN 0-87614-966-2). Paperback. Adams chose photography over music, building wilderness support.

Think Like an Eagle: At Work With a Wildlife Photographer by Kathryn Lasky. (ISBN 0-316-51519-1). The author discovers that taking pictures of wildlife isn't easy.

When the Wolves Return by Ron Hirschi. (ISBN 0-525-65144-6). Poetic text, with spectacular color photographs by Tom Mangelson, focused on helping the wolf survive.

Polar the Titanic Bear by Daisy Spedden. (ISBN 0-316-80625-0). Family photos and beautiful illustrations tell of a young survivor of the Titanic and his white stuffed bear.

Turn of the Century: Our Nation 100 Years Ago by Nancy Smiler Levinson. (ISBN 0-525-67433-0). A photographic view of the turn of last century.

John Muir: Wilderness Prophet by Peter Anderson. (ISBN 0-531-15781-4). Paperback.

Keep the Rest of the Class Reading and Writing ... While You Teach Small Groups   Scholastic Professional Books

Finding Information in a Photograph

Describe who is in the picture.

What is happening? What was being said and done before the picture was taken?

Where and when was this picture taken? (Conjecture is O.K.)

Why do you think the picture was taken? Why was it chosen for this book?

If you were the subject of this picture, what would you be thinking?

Describe something of particular interest to you in this picture.

Writing at Centers

Writing as a Literacy-Focused Activity

for Small Groups

To improve as writers, students need both instruction and frequent practice in a variety of writing experiences. Literacy centers are ideal for this practice. Children need to know how to read content, take notes, and communicate information. They need writing to generate and clarify thinking. The following ideas, which focus on the connection between writing and reading, are designed for center work and for small group work within the center rotation.

▸▸ **WHO IS GUTZON BORGLUM?** is a literacy center example of how a nonfiction selection can be used to generate personal responses. The FACTS AND COMMENTARY ABOUT form provides a place for students to state facts gleaned from reading and then respond with their own commentary. Students can use more than one form if they run out of space.

▸▸ **TAKE YOUR PICK: ONE HUNDRED JOURNAL TOPICS** uses personal experience as a prompt for writing—consider incorporating it into the center rotation as a choice activity. Many teachers have students return to their journals at a later date in order to work on writing skills by expanding upon the autobiographical entries.

▸▸ **"KING OF THE SKY"** is a nonfiction selection paired with PANEL DISCUSSION. It is used to demonstrate how an interesting topic can generate a panel discussion (an oral language, literacy-focused activity for a small group). The "practical" writing is filling out the form and putting one's questions on index cards. I have used this exercise successfully with students as young as third grade, with each student happily responsible for filling out the "official" form. With "King of the Sky," panel members each take a paragraph as their topic and create three or four questions that they will be prepared to answer. Even though panel members create the questions they are to be asked and have the answers prepared ahead of time, a surprising amount of learning occurs.

▸▸ **AGREE, DISAGREE** is a literacy center activity that invites students to agree or disagree with a mildly controversial statement related to literature that is currently being read or to subject matter being studied. Students copy the statement onto a sheet of paper and state whether they agree or disagree; then they offer at least five facts to support their position. Suggestions for statements to be posted at the center include:

- It was a good thing that the BFG kidnapped Sophie.
- Native Americans had the right to attack settlers.
- Friendship is the theme of *Charlotte's Web*.
- Sam should have told his father about the swans.

▸▸ **MRS. PIGGLE-WIGGLE** illustrates how chapter titles can be used to build summarizing skills. Use this idea with any chapter book.

Students may work on this independently as a choice activity during centers rotation, or a small group reading the same book may work on it together. A variation on this, and as a center activity for any chapter book or novel that is being read, is to have children write a brief summary of the chapter along with a small illustration on an index card. The cards may be hole-punched and tied together with yarn or put on a ring.

This idea works well with nonfiction books too. Have students practice note taking skills by using chapter titles (if the chapters are brief) or the sections delineated by bolded sub-titles (if they are not) as the topic for each index card. Allow students to work in small groups to find key facts in each chapter or bolded section. As a small-group literacy-focused activity, the novelty of working together builds interest, and reinforcing content information can easily become part of the classroom rotation. Be sure to provide guided practice before expecting students to do this independently.

PAGE 40

▸▸ A TELEPHONE POEM is fun and useful at all grade levels. Children write their telephone number at the top of the page, and each number reflects the number of words per line. (Zero can be zero or ten.) Use this format to summarize a field trip, report on a book, comment on a science experiment, describe artwork, or focus on a particular topic under study.

844-7358

Tidepools have lots of animals living in them.
Tidepools are very wet.
Animals live in tidepools.
Tidepools are calm with lots of life.
Creatures in water.
A world in a world.
Nature's beauty in a tidepool world is spectacular.

PAGE 41

▸▸ READ ALL ABOUT IT! is a novelty page, the novelty being the newspaper format. This is a literacy center activity that asks students to summarize the plot of a book they've read, to give their opinion about the book, and to profile the major character. If several students have read the same book, or even the same story, this easily becomes a small-group literacy-focused activity. Summarizing, editorializing, and describing a character are all skills that can be practiced at this center.

PAGE 42

▸▸ THE GENERAL WRITING RUBRIC has been used successfully in a number of classrooms. It has been adapted and adjusted to clarify teacher expectations and work across grade levels.

▸▸ CAMERA IN THE CLASSROOM is an open-ended literacy center. There is no worksheet. Photographs are simply used as writing prompts. This complements the activity in which photographs in books were studied. Students may be asked to create titles, captions, or stories for photographs posted at a center. Field trips, science experiments, and oral reports are all potential photo opportunities. A photograph becomes the basis for practice with descriptive writing that focuses on personal feelings, reactions, and attention to sensory detail (see Chapter 8, "Genre Studies"). Children enjoy writing about themselves and about each other. A class photo album with labels provides caption-writing opportunities. Students should write a first draft and have it corrected before writing in the album.

Who Is Gutzon Borglum?

Gutzon Borglum spent the last 14 years of his life creating the world's most gigantic sculpture. It is one of the manmade wonders of the world, and 360 workers participated in its creation. Do you know what it is?

In the Black Hills of South Dakota, near the geographic center of the continental United States, are four faces carved into a granite mountain—the faces of George Washington, Thomas Jefferson, Abraham Lincoln, and Teddy Roosevelt. They were shaped by dynamite, jackhammers, air hammers, and steel wedges. Eight million pounds of stone were removed from the mountain in the process.

Mount Rushmore National Memorial is visited each year by over two million people who can view Borglum's four granite faces 5,725 feet above sea level. They are not hard to see, as each bust is taller even than the great Sphinx of Egypt. From chin to the top of the head, the faces alone are 60 feet tall. Borglum, the son of Danish immigrants, was determined to demonstrate his love for his country and wanted to mirror the magnitude of nature. He said, "...volume shocks the nerve or soul centers and is emotional in its effect."

Borglum worked in a studio at the base of the mountain and sculpted models to guide the carving. If the carving time alone were calculated, it took six-and-a-half years of carving to form the faces, but bad weather and lack of money slowed progress. Another delay was caused when the Thomas Jefferson sculpture, which was originally begun on Washington's right side, had to be started again after a year-and-a-half of carving when the workers hit rock that couldn't be worked.

Borglum, who began Mount Rushmore in 1927 when he was 60 years old, died at the age of 74 before he could finish carving the figures to their waists. His son, Lincoln, also a sculptor, completed the Mount Rushmore project. Called America's "Shrine of Democracy," it is an awe-inspiring patriotic statement in stone, created because of Gutzon Borglum's determination to symbolize the birth and growth of America in a big way.

Facts and Commentary About:

_____

Fact:

Comment:

Fact:

Comment:

Fact:

Comment:

Fact:

Comment:

Take Your Pick: One Hundred Journal Topics

Directions: You may choose any of the following topics. Check off each one as it is chosen. Write the topic as a title for your journal entry, skip a line, indent, and begin writing.

- ☐ What I Like To Do On Weekends
- ☐ Something I Can Do Now That I Couldn't Do Last Year
- ☐ How I Helped Someone Once
- ☐ Something I Am Proud Of
- ☐ The People I'd Invite To My Birthday Party
- ☐ The Clothes I Need
- ☐ What My Bedroom Looks Like
- ☐ What The Inside Of Our Refrigerator Looks Like
- ☐ What I Would Put On A Sign That Would Go On My Bedroom Door
- ☐ Someone In My Family That I Really Like
- ☐ Somewhere I Like To Go With My Family
- ☐ A Sport I Like To Watch
- ☐ One Of My Friends
- ☐ A Time I Got Into Trouble
- ☐ A Trip I've Taken
- ☐ A Pet I Have (or A Pet I'd Like To Have)
- ☐ How I Would Change The World To Make It Better
- ☐ Someone I'd Take On A Trip
- ☐ What I Do When I'm Angry
- ☐ What I Do When I'm Frightened
- ☐ The Best Teacher I've Ever Had

- ☐ How I Would Spend $5,000.00
- ☐ A Time I Was Embarrassed
- ☐ A Time My Feelings Were Hurt
- ☐ What I Would Be Doing Right Now If I Could Do Anything I Wanted
- ☐ What I Think About When I Can't Fall Asleep
- ☐ What My Favorite Song Is And Why
- ☐ What I Like About Myself
- ☐ A Talent I Wish I Had
- ☐ The Last Time I Cried And Why
- ☐ What Makes My Life Complicated
- ☐ Three Things I'd Take With Me If I Moved
- ☐ What Makes Me Laugh
- ☐ An Animal I'd Like To Be
- ☐ A Trophy I'd Like To Win
- ☐ A Store I'd Like To Own
- ☐ How I Feel About Earthquakes
- ☐ How I Feel About Rain
- ☐ How I Feel About Snow
- ☐ The Best Thing That Has Ever Happened To Me
- ☐ The Worst Thing That Has Ever Happened To Me
- ☐ Something I Hope Will Happen To Me

- The Color I Think Of When I'm Happy
- What I Would Like To Be Famous For
- The Best Birthday Present I Ever Got
- My Feelings About Television
- My Feelings About Fast Food
- My Feelings About Junk Food
- My Favorite Meal
- How I Feel About Pollution
- A Discussion About Good Manners
- A Description Of Myself
- Something That Is Boring
- Something That Is Exciting
- How I Got My Name And How I Feel About It
- My Friends
- Three Wishes
- Reasons For A Messy Desk
- Reasons For A Neat Desk
- Remembering Kindergarten
- Remembering First Grade
- Remembering Second Grade
- Three Excuses For Not Eating My Lunch
- My Least Favorite Food
- The Most Important Subject In School
- The Least Important Subject In School
- Why I Want To Go To College
- The Hardest Job I've Ever Had
- The Kinds Of Books I Like To Read
- Why I Save Money
- Why I Don't Save Money

- Things I've Learned From Television
- Things I've Learned From Books
- Something I've Learned From Talking To Someone
- How I Wake Up In The Morning
- Someone I'd Like To Know Better
- My Skills In The Kitchen
- Something I'm Curious About
- Sounds I Like And Don't Like
- A Good Dream
- A Bad Dream
- What I'd Do If I Were Invisible
- What I'd Do If Everyone Forgot My Birthday
- A Surprise Phone Call
- Being Sick
- The Reason For Rainbows
- Why The Ocean Is Salty
- How Cats Got Whiskers
- My Favorite Place
- Promises
- The Funniest Thing That Has Ever Happened To Me
- The Weirdest Thing That Has Ever Happened To Me
- Strange Sounds
- Ten Years From Now
- A Wonderful Person Whom I Know
- When I Am A Parent
- Homework
- Sports I Enjoy Watching
- A Time When I Was Scolded

King of the Sky

For thousands of years, the eagle has been a symbol of power and strength. He was worshipped as a god by the Mesopotamians (Mesopotamia is now Iraq) and common in the art of the Persians, Chaldeans, and Egyptians. The Sumerians even believed that the eagle brought their children. The eagle was the symbol of Greece in the fourth century BC, at the time of Alexander the Great, and the symbol of Napoleon's France. The Romans had eagles on their military flags to symbolize courage and bravery.

Many Plains Indians, such as the Sioux, wore eagle feathers as a sign of bravery and decorated their shields, weapons, and war bonnets with them. The Hopi Indians of the southwest raided eagles' nests and kept eagles for their feathers. The birds were attached to the housetop and fed mice and rabbits, making the feathers easily available. The markings on the feathers were thought to have been caused by rain, so when these desert dwellers did their rain dances, they felt the feathers were especially valuable.

The image of the bald eagle on the Great Seal of the United States is there because the bald eagle is the national bird of the United States. Benjamin Franklin did not think that the bald eagle should be our national bird; he wanted the turkey for our symbol. He thought the eagle was lazy and cowardly and that it was really a foreign bird. Franklin was outvoted by the other founding fathers because they saw the eagle as noble and proud, a good representative for a new nation defying its old rulers.

The bald eagle is also known as the American eagle, and it is really not bald. It has white feathers on its head and neck. Unlike the golden eagle, the bald eagle has no feathers on its lower legs. It lives near lakes, rivers, and coastal areas, but ranges from Canada and Alaska in the north to Florida in the east and Baja California in the west. Its diet consists mostly of fish, but it doesn't always do its own hunting. Compared to other eagles, the bald eagle is somewhat clumsy. It attacks other birds for their fish and also eats dead fish. Bald eagles are diurnal, which means that they fly and hunt during the day.

Eagles build their nests, called aeries, at the top of tall trees, sometimes more than 80 feet above the ground. Sometimes their nests are on cliff ledges, but they are always high so that the eagles can be on the lookout for prey. It is believed that eagles mate for life and, once built, a nest may be used by the same pair of eagles year after year. A pair of eagles may take four to six weeks to build their nest, which is usually five to eight feet high and wide. Stories have been told of eagles' nests which have been 20 feet deep and 10 feet across. A nest in Ohio was found to weigh 4,000 pounds.

Eagles hatch and raise only one or two nestlings a year, and habitat disturbances have threatened many species. The bald eagle, in particular, has been endangered for many years, but seems to be making a comeback and thus able to keep the title, "King of the Sky"

Name: _____

Panel Discussion

A good way to share what you have learned about a topic is to hold a panel discussion. List the names of those who will be working together on this panel:

1. _____ **3.** _____

2. _____ **4.** _____

What is your topic?

_____

Once the topic has been selected, each panel member must choose a specific part of the topic and become an "expert" in that area. (That may mean more research and information.) Write the name of the panel member and his/her subject area:

1. _____

2. _____

3. _____

4. _____

The moderator's job is to organize the panel's questions and have enough background information to keep the discussion going smoothly. Who will be your moderator?

_____

Write down the questions you will be prepared to answer.

1. _____

_____

2. _____

_____

3. _____

_____

4. _____

_____

5. _____

_____

Teacher approval of questions: _____(teacher's initials)

Make a copy of your questions for the moderator. Use one index card for each question.

Be sure that you have a copy of your questions and answers so you can practice.

When will your panel be ready to present its discussion? _____

How much time will your group need? _____

The moderator will assemble all the questions from the panel members. The moderator may ask the questions or distribute the questions to audience members. At the end of the discussion, the moderator may briefly sum up what the members of the group have said.

It's important to practice with your group ahead of time. Write down one or two practice dates below:

_____   _____

How did your group do? Evaluate your panel discussion. What worked? What didn't work? How can you improve it?

_____

_____

_____

_____

Agree, Disagree

Statement:

☐ I agree.

☐ I disagree.

Here's Why:

1. _____

_____

_____

2. _____

_____

_____

3. _____

_____

_____

4. _____

_____

_____

5. _____

_____

_____

Mrs. Piggle-Wiggle

by Betty MacDonald

Mrs. Piggle-Wiggle lives in a wonderful upside-down house and knows everything about children. She uses her imagination and common sense to cure problems. Describe her cure next to each chapter title; then, create a chapter title for an imaginary chapter (nine) and tell about a problem you'd like to solve. Write your idea for a cure to that problem.

Chapter 1: "Mrs. Piggle-Wiggle Herself"

_____

_____

_____

Chapter 2: "The Won't-Pick-Up-Toys Cure"

_____

_____

_____

_____

Chapter 3: "The Answer-Backer Cure"

_____

_____

_____

_____

Chapter 4: "The Selfishness Cure"

_____

_____

_____

_____

Chapter 5: "The Radish Cure"

_____

_____

_____

Chapter 6: "The Never-Want-To-Go-To-Bedders Cure"

_____

_____

_____

_____

_____

Chapter 7: "The Slow-Eater-Tiny-Bite-Taker Cure"

_____

_____

_____

_____

_____

Chapter 8: "The Fighter-Quarrelers Cure"

_____

_____

_____

_____

_____

Chapter 9: _____

_____

_____

_____

_____

_____

A Telephone Poem

My Phone Number:

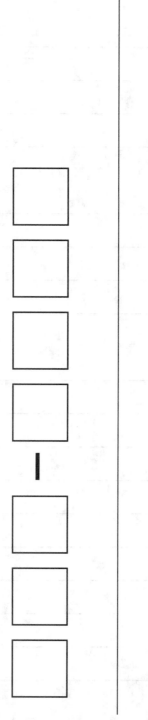

The number of words in each line of your poem will depend on your telephone number. If your phone number is 555-1212, the first line of your poem will have five words, and so on.

Read All About It!

Volume 1, Issue 1

Feature Story:

The plot thickens!
Reader tells all!
Learn the story behind
the story!

Editorial:

What did the reader
really think about this
book?

Profile:

Who was the key
character?
Discover why!

Keep the Rest of the Class Reading and Writing ... While You Teach Small Groups   Scholastic Professional Books

General Writing Rubric

Name: _____ **Date:** _____

Assignment: _____

4 Excellent

- ☐ Punctuation is correct.
- ☐ Spelling is correct.
- ☐ Sentences are clear and have complete thoughts.
- ☐ Paragraphs are identified, indented, and organized with topic sentences or by dialogue.
- ☐ Descriptive words and details are used in sentences and paragraphs.
- ☐ Information is neatly presented, reflecting personal pride.

3 Good

- ☐ There are very few punctuation errors.
- ☐ There are very few spelling mistakes
- ☐ Most sentences are clear and have complete thoughts.
- ☐ Most paragraphs are identified, indented, and have good organization using topic sentences or dialogue.
- ☐ Descriptive words and details are generally used in sentences and paragraphs.
- ☐ Information is neatly presented.

2 Satisfactory

- ☐ There are occasional punctuation mistakes.
- ☐ There are occasional spelling mistakes.
- ☐ Most sentences have complete thoughts.
- ☐ Some paragraphs are not organized, identified, or indented
- ☐ Descriptive words and details are used in some sentences.
- ☐ Information is presentable.

1 Unatisfactory

- ☐ Most punctuation is incorrect or missing.
- ☐ There are many spelling mistakes.
- ☐ Many sentences are fragments, run-ons, or unclear.
- ☐ Paragraphs are not organized, identified, or indented.
- ☐ Sentences have little detail or description.
- ☐ Information is not neatly presented.

Comments: _____

_____

Thank you to Terri Gootgeld Carter for sharing this multi-use rubric.

CHAPTER 4

Noticing What Authors Do

"Noticing" what an author does has two distinct benefits: Students' writing skills improve, and appreciation for the written word is nurtured. Here are some ideas for teaching what needs to be "noticed" about story structure, vocabulary, and style and format.

STORY STRUCTURE

Picture books provide a model for introducing story structure, because the beginning, middle, and ending are identified easily. Picture books put children in touch with excellent literature and demonstrate the author's craft. They are powerful models for children's writing because students can see how stories are structured.

PAGE 44
▸▸ Use the STORY STRUCTURE WEB to teach the elements of story structure. In most picture books the author lays the groundwork for the story by beginning with a succinctly presented problem. The middle of the book often finds the main character in a situation where things keep getting worse. When the story ends, things have changed. Students should look back to the problem the author presented in the beginning.

PAGE 45
▸▸ CHOOSE FOUR: A FOCUS ON BEGINNINGS provides a center activity sheet which helps students focus on story beginnings.

PAGE 46
▸▸ TAKE THE LEAD presents five kinds of leads and asks students to find examples.

PAGE 48
▸▸ WHAT A CHARACTER! When asked to describe the characters in the books they read, children are often at a loss for words—literally! They simply do not know the vocabulary to describe inner qualities or character traits. These two pages provide lists of words to help students think and write sentences about the characters in their books. As an advanced exercise have your students turn their sentences into paragraphs.

PAGE 50
▸▸ Creating a CHARACTER TRAITS CLUSTER begins with the character's name in the center oval. Students add adjectives to the spokes extending from the oval to describe characters.

VOCABULARY

PAGE 51
▸▸ A VOCABULARY MENU: APPETIZER, MAIN COURSE, DESSERT offers students choices as they investigate the author's use of words.

PAGE 52
▸▸ WORD SORTING FOR VOCABULARY BUILDING lets students put words into categories to practice and reinforce skills. The examples include *Abel's Island*, which focuses on vocabulary building, and *Hog-Eye*, which focuses more on word structure. Arm your students with dictionaries and allow them to work collaboratively. They'll discover categories you haven't even considered. Word study makes sense when the vocabulary is worth a second look.

STYLE AND FORMAT

PAGE 55
▸▸ SETTING THE SCENE introduces the device of changing the place and/or time to change the action and leads the way towards further exploration of the way scenes are used in the books students are reading.

Keep the Rest of the Class Reading and Writing ... While You Teach Small Groups   Scholastic Professional Books

Story Structure Web

In the web below, write the title of the book you've read. Write three facts about the beginning, middle, and end of your book.

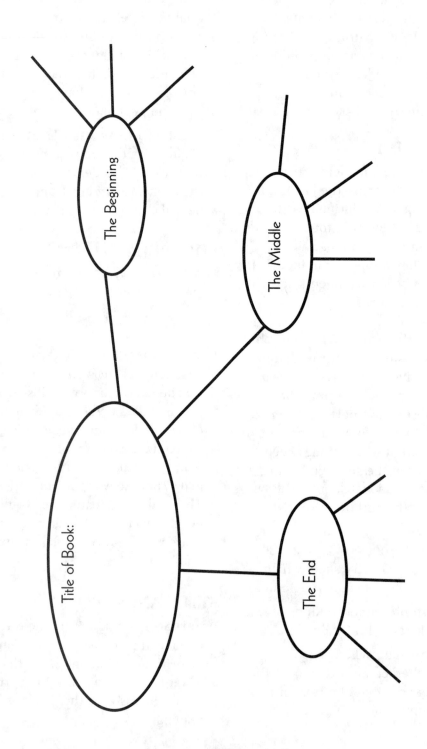

Title of Book:

The Beginning

The Middle

The End

Choose Four: A Focus on Beginnings

Choose **four** of the picture books at this center and read the beginning of each book. Pay attention to how each story begins: Authors want readers to be interested, so they usually start their stories with a lead sentence or two that will make you want to read more.

Write the titles and the authors of the four books whose beginnings you read.

1.
Title: _____

Author: _____

2.
Title: _____

Author: _____

3.
Title: _____

Author: _____

4.
Title: _____

Author: _____

Now...
Put an asterisk (*) by the title of the book that has your favorite beginning lines; then, read the rest of the book.

Respond to the following on another sheet of paper. Attach it to this sheet.

1. Write down the important beginning sentences.

2. Why were they so important?

3. What information did the author give you?

4. Tell a little about the middle of the story and tell how the end relates back to the beginning.

Take the Lead

Leads are the first words that you read when you begin a book. They are written to get your attention and keep you reading. Authors use different kinds of leads. There are five kinds described below. At this center, you will look for an example of each of the different kinds of leads. Write the lead line(s) you find in their appropriate category and the book's title in the next column. An example is given for each category.

Kind of Lead	Lead Lines	Book Title
SETTING LEAD (tells where or when the story takes place)	Ex. My great-aunt Arizona was born in a log cabin her papa built in the meadow on Henson Creek in the Blue Ridge Mountains.	*My Great-Aunt Arizona* by Gloria Houston
CHARACTER LEAD (describes the character)	Ex. Mrs. Gorf had a long tongue and pointed ears.	*Sideways Stories From Wayside School* by Louis Sachar
DIALOGUE LEAD (someone's talking)	Ex. "Where's Papa going with that ax?"	*Charlotte's Web* by E.B. White

Kind of Lead	Lead Lines	Book Title
ACTION LEAD (something's happening)	Ex. Walking back to camp through the swamp, Sam wondered whether to tell his father what he had seen.	*The Trumpet of the Swan* by E.B. White
SUMMARY LEAD (answers who, what, where, when, and why)	Ex. David often wondered about how he happened to be sitting there on the stair landing, within arm's reach of the headless cupid, at the very moment when his stepmother left Westerly House to bring Amanda home.	*The Headless Cupid* by Zilpha Keatley Snyder

Which kind of lead do you think is the most effective?

_____

_____

Which lead made you want to read the book?

_____

_____

What a Character! (1)

Book Title: _____

Character's Name: _____

Circle six of the character traits listed below which you think best describe the character you've named. On a separate sheet of paper define each trait. Below each definition write a sentence that uses the word and explains why it describes the character. (An example from the book *Frindle* by Andrew Clements would be: *Nick was* **inventive** *when he created a new word for a pen.*) Staple this sheet to the page with your sentences.

eager	easy-going
efficient	energetic
enthusiastic	fair
firm	flexible
forgiving	frank
friendly	generous
gentle	good-natured
healthy	helpful
honest	hopeful
humble	humorous
imaginative	independent
individualistic	industrious
intelligent	inventive
kind	likable

Keep the Rest of the Class Reading and Writing ... While You Teach Small Groups   Scholastic Professional Books

What a Character! (2)

Book Title: _____

Character's Name: _____

Circle six of the character traits listed below which you think best describe the character you've named. On a separate sheet of paper define each trait. Below each definition write a sentence that uses the word and explains why it describes the character. (Example: _Sweet Clara was_ **resourceful** _when she used bits of leftover cloth to create the quilt._) Staple this sheet to the page with your sentences.

logical	loyal
methodical	modest
motivated	open-minded
optimistic	practical
precise	prudent
purposeful	realistic
reliable	resourceful
responsible	self-confident
sensible	serious
sincere	sociable
spontaneous	strong-willed
tenacious	thorough
trustworthy	versatile
wary	witty

Keep the Rest of the Class Reading and Writing ... While You Teach Small Groups   Scholastic Professional Books

Character Traits Cluster

What important character has the author of your book created? What traits make the character important to the plot? Put the character's name in the oval at the center of the cluster. Add adjectives at the end of the spokes to describe the character. Add more spokes if you need them. Be able to justify your choices.

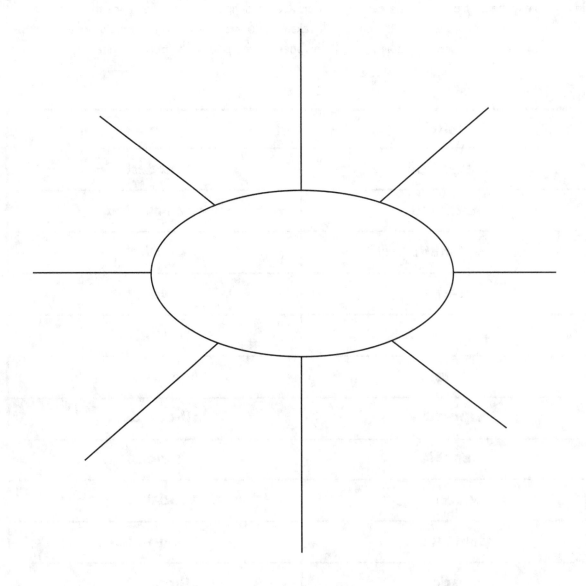

Book Title: _____

Your Name: _____

A Vocabulary Menu: Appetizer, Main Course, Dessert

Authors choose their words very carefully. Some authors challenge readers by using sesquipedalian words (words with many syllables). Some authors use words to create scenes or pictures in your mind. Some authors just like to "play" with words, using alliteration or puns to make the text fun to read. For this activity, choose a book with interesting vocabulary (books by William Steig, E.B. White, or Roald Dahl are particularly good) and complete three activities from this menu. Choose one from the "Appetizer" column, one from the "Main Course" column, and one from the "Dessert" column.

Appetizer	Main Course	Dessert
❏ Create a crossword puzzle using at least 20 interesting vocabulary words from your book. Don't forget to provide the clues.	❏ How many sesquipedalian words can you find? (For this activity, they should have three syllables or more.) When you have found at least 10, use each one in a sentence about yourself.	❏ Look for examples of word play. These can include puns, the use of humor, alliteration, and onomatopoeia. Write down at least five and discuss how it felt as a reader to encounter a "playful" author.
❏ Create a word search containing at least 20 sesquipedalian words. Trade your word search with someone else who created one.	❏ Chapter titles often reflect the story's setting, an element of the plot, a story character, a story event, or emotions felt. Are there titles for each of the chapters in your book? If there are, discuss the reasons you think the author chose those titles. Is there any kind of pattern to the naming of the chapters? If there are no titles, you are to create them.	❏ Authors appeal to the senses when they write descriptively. The author may tell you about what you'd see, hear, smell, feel, or even taste. Choose three separate selections and tell why you feel each is an example of excellent descriptive writing.

Word Sorting for Vocabulary Building

Word sorting is a strategy developed by Patricia Cunningham for putting words into categories in order to practice or reinforce specific skills. This technique was designed to be used in small, homogeneous guided reading groups, but it works effectively at a center and can be "tweaked" to focus on vocabulary building. Known words should form the basis for the sort early in reading development, but vocabulary growth can be a focus with students more advanced in their literacy evolution.

Words can be sorted by number of syllables, how letters represent sounds (alliteration, rime), by the patterns letters make in words (the placement of consonants and vowels, how that grouping dictates pronunciation), and by concepts (meaning, parts of speech, categories). The use of the dictionary is mandatory when meaning is one of the options for sorting. Interest is higher when words being sorted come from familiar literature or a content area being studied.

Ideas for word sorting:

☐ Rhyming words
☐ Words that are proper nouns
☐ Words with suffixes
☐ Words with prefixes
☐ Words with common onsets (beginning consonant elements, blends, digraphs)
☐ Words with common rimes (the vowel and what follows)
☐ Words with common vowel patterns
☐ Words derived from the same base word
☐ Words of one, two, or three syllables
☐ Words that double consonants, words that don't
☐ Words that are nouns, adjectives, verbs (parts of speech)
☐ Words that are compound words
☐ Words whose past tense is completely different than their present tense (taught-teach)
☐ Words according to subject area
☐ Words whose meanings establish categories.

A previous readaloud is a good choice since it provides a meaning "connection." The word sort that follows is based on William Steig's book *Abel's Island*, a great readaloud appropriate for fifth or sixth grade. A second word sort is based on the picture book *Hog-Eye*, by Susan Meddaugh.

Your third graders may want to cut out the words and work silently as they try to figure out the categories, but older students may just check words off and create lists on a separate sheet of paper. Initially you may want to begin with a key word for each category to guide the sorting and instill the comparison analogy as students match their choices. Students who are sorting for vocabulary building are also building dictionary skills, an added advantage of the process.

Keep the Rest of the Class Reading and Writing ... While You Teach Small Groups   Scholastic Professional Books

A Word Sort: *Abel's Island*

by William Steig

sorrow	abominable	plummeted	disappointment
regret	perilous	somnolent	misery
frivolous	skedaddled	prehistoric	loving
ecstasy	miraculous	ambled	foundered
terror	resentment	indignant	equinoctial
inescapable	unfearing	calm	indulgent
foisted	amassing	overwhelmed	apprehension
smugness	proliferated	meditative	anguish
confusion	tenderness	illumined	garnered

A Word Sort: *Hog-Eye*

by Susan Meddaugh

whole	true	big
wish	make	getting
came	calmly	sooner
reader	decided	grabbed
limped	working	stalling
fortunately	everywhere	crankily
cookbook	threeleaf	finally
singing	exactly	underwear
scared	sack	cried

Setting the Scene

Stories have to begin somewhere. The author decides where the story will take place, but because stories have to have things happen, the author often changes the place or the time of day. Changing the place or time in a story sets the scene for new action to occur. In the book *Charlotte's Web*, the author, E.B. White, used location changes and the time of day to create reasons for different events to occur.

For this center, you may use either a picture book or the chapter book you are reading. Identify at least four scene changes. Write the title of the book and the author, where the story began, where it moved to, and what action occurred when the author changed the scene.

Title: _____

Author: _____

Scene	Action

Author Studies

Good teaching requires a good sales technique. We are "selling" when we devise strategies to create interest in books and when we share our fascination with an author's life and the books he has written. I've discovered that a love of books is contagious and that motivation on a grand scale can be achieved with author studies.

Author Hall of Fame

This is not a center, but a literacy-focused activity for a small group. This collaborative activity is designed to mesh with center rotation time. Each small group will create a bulletin board to honor an author for the books that author has written. The bulletin board is the focal point of this author study.

Planning time is necessary for this activity. You may wish to assign specific due dates with each group's display being left up for a designated period of time. (Remember to use the Group Planning Sheet!)

An author biography is integral to this project. Biographies can be accessed on the Internet or in a number of recent books. A sampling of the author's books should be displayed.

Students can highlight an author's books in a variety of ways. "Hall of Fame" activities might include:

✓ panel discussions
✓ excerpts read aloud
✓ reading the flyleaf
✓ dramatization of a scene
✓ crossword puzzles
✓ "booktalks" for individual books
    (a short talk to "sell" the book).
✓ created book covers
✓ role playing an interview with the
    author
✓ corresponding with the author

Hall of Fame "Possibilities"

Arnold Lobel
Chris Van Allsburg
Paul Goble
Maurice Sendak
Ezra Jack Keats
William Steig
Verna Aardema
Roald Dahl
Jane Yolen
John Steptoe
Faith Ringgold
Betsy Byars
Scott O'Dell
Elizabeth George Speare
Madeleine L'Engle
E.L. Konigsburg
Judy Blume
Katherine Paterson
Beverly Cleary
Charlotte Zolotow
Judith Viorst
Patricia Polacco
Steven Kellogg
E.B. White
Robert Kimmel Smith
...and many, many more!

Author Hall of Fame: Group Planning Sheet

Name: _____

Students working with you on this project:

Name of author:

Books written by your author:

Bulletin board due date:

Check off each responsibility as it is completed:

- ☐ Plan the bulletin board
- ☐ Artwork for the bulletin board
- ☐ Author biography
- ☐ Book display
- ☐ Group presentation (e.g., panel discussion, booktalks, book covers, role play)
- ☐ Class activities (e.g., crossword puzzle, author biography questions, word search)

Group presentation due date:

Class activities due date:

Notes _____

_____

_____

_____

Take a close look at an author who has written several books or series. Authors who fall into this category include Bruce Coville, Barbara Park, Brian Jacques, Peg Kehret, Ben Mikaelsen, Louis Sacher, and Beverly Cleary.

An Author Profile of _____

List the titles of three books that you have read by this author. Use the numbers of the titles to fill in the chart.

1. _____

2. _____

3. _____

What genre is this book? (fantasy, realistic fiction, mystery, humor, science fiction...)	Describe the protagonist (the main character, sometimes the hero) in the story.
1.	1.
2.	2.
3.	3.

An Author Profile (Continued)

What is the main conflict in this story? (person vs. person, person vs. beast, person vs. the forces of nature, person vs. himself, person vs. fate...)	What did the author do to get you involved in this story? (What made you keep reading and what kept you interested?)
1.	1.
2.	2.
3.	3.

Would you recommend this author to a friend?   Why?

Allen Say: A Study of An Author / Illustrator

Locate at least three of the books named below. Read them carefully. Put checks in the appropriate categories.

BOOK TITLE	There was a journey.	Asian and American cultures were important to the story.	A respect for the environment was shown.	There was fantasy.	The importance of family was part of the story.
Grandfather's Journey					
The Bicycle Man					
How My Parents Learned to Eat					
The Lost Lake					
Allison					
The Boy of the Three-Year Nap					
A River Dream					
Tree of Cranes					
Stranger in the Mirror					
Under the Cherry Blossom Tree					

61

Author Study: The Picture Books of Kevin Henkes

BOOK TITLE	Animals act like people.	There is a problem and it is solved.	There is humor.	The illustrations help tell the story.	There is a family in the story.	There is a happy ending.	The back cover tells more of the story.
Chester's Way							
Chrysanthemum							
Grandpa & Bo							
Jessica							
Julius, the Baby of the World							
Lily's Purple Plastic Purse							
Owen							
Sheila Rae, the Brave							
A Weekend with Wendell							

Which of Kevin Henkes' books was your favorite?

What is there about this author that you especially like?

William Steig's Animal Fantasies

Circle the book you'll use for this activity:

Sylvester and the Magic Pebble   Amos and Boris

Shrek!   Gorky Rises

The Amazing Bone

Dr. DeSoto Goes to Africa

What makes an animal story an animal fantasy? In animal fantasies, animals act like humans. They talk, have friends, wear clothes, and still may behave at times like animals. Most animal fantasies have more than one animal character that is important to the story. Use the animal characters in your book to fill in the chart.

Name of Character	In what ways did this animal character act human?	What animal characteristics did this character have?

What was the lesson to be learned in this story?

Weather, Whales, Wolves, and Wildfires

Seymour Simon, Nonfiction Author

Seymour Simon writes nonfiction books about everything: space, dinosaurs, optical illusions, oceans, earthquakes, volcanoes, snakes, sharks, the heart, the brain—you name it. At this center, you will be looking through several of Simon's books. Choose three books about topics that interest you and read them. When you've finished, write down the titles of those books. Under each title, create five questions based on the information in the book. Write down the questions below each title. Answer the questions on a separate sheet of paper.

Title:
1.
2.
3.
4.
5.

Title:
1.
2.
3.
4.
5.

Title:

1.

2.

3.

4.

5.

Summarize the book you enjoyed the most. Write a five-sentence paragraph. In the first sentence, tell the title of the book. In the next three sentences, tell three things you learned. In the last sentence, explain why this book was the one you liked best.

_____

_____

_____

_____

_____

_____

_____

_____

_____

_____

_____

_____

_____

Author Activities: A Menu

Directions: Choose three of the six activities. Check off each activity as it is completed.

☐ Read the biography of one of the authors featured at this center. Read each paragraph carefully. What questions did the interviewer ask? Write down at least eight questions that the author had to answer so that the interviewer would have this information.

☐ Choose one of your favorite authors. Using the list of character traits, create a cluster around that author's name and write down the traits that the author possesses. With that information, write a paragraph describing your author.

☐ Read two books by the same author. Try an author whose books you have never read before. They can be picture books or chapter books. Prepare a chart to compare and contrast similarities and differences in the characters, the setting, the theme, and the plot.

☐ Design a "Which Author?" test about your favorite author. The questions can be about the subject matter or genre of the books, the literary devices the author uses, or they may be questions you ask from information about the author's life. Formulate 20 questions. (Don't forget to keep a copy of the answers!)

☐ Create a chart or diagram with the names of five authors whose biographies you can read at this center. Read about the details in their lives. Look for common events in their lives. What experiences did they share? Where did they grow up? How do they describe their childhood and going to school? What about their families? Show this information on your chart.

☐ Think about an author you really like. Turn each of the following phrases into sentences about that author:

I can't decide if...

If I had to choose...

It seems important to note...

If one of this author's books was a movie...

One criticism is...

I have discovered that...

I would like to ask...

I want to read...

Using the Internet for Author Studies

Cyberspace offers a smorgasbord of à la carte opportunities to enrich and support your reading program. Your computer can also be used simply as the delivery system for information you can use at centers. Here are some great Web sites that will provide author biographies and thematic literature units to complement author studies.

- Kay Vandergrift's home page is a well-known site for over 500 links to authors and illustrators. The extensive list of sites provides biographical and autobiographical author information. http://www.scils.rutgers.edu/special/kay/author.html.

- The Schools of California On-line Resources for Education (SCORE) home page is at http://www.score.k12.ca.us. CyberGuides contain thematic units that cross genres, provide Web connections to authors and related topics, and evaluation rubrics.

- Aaron Shepard writes wonderful Readers' Theater scripts. He graciously allows his Web site visitors to download and print entire scripts in a variety of genres. Use the scripts for performance, for genre study work, and use Aaron's personal information for an author study. You can visit him at http://www.aaronshep.com/rt/RTE.html.

- The Cooperative Children's Book Center at http://www.soemadison.wisc.edu/ccbc/ is an esoteric and unique resource. You can access annotated bibliographies and download lists such as "Thirty Multicultural Books Every Child Should Know." Use the bibliographies to help plan specific thematic studies as well as author studies.

- An all-time favorite is David Brown's Web site. He lists children's book awards from around the world, updates the Newbery and Caldecott winners, lists Best Books, comments on them, and maintains the *Web Travelers Toolkit* which has innumerable other links. There are many author links and links to author links http://www.acs.ucalgary.ca/~dkbrown/

- Carol Hurst's Children's Literature Site, http://www.carolhurst.com, is another great find. When a book is reviewed on this site, the "Things to Notice and Talk About" section provides outstanding teaching ideas to enrich author studies. Special sections include "Picture Books for the Upper Grades" and annotated thematic book lists.

- Fairrosa Cyber Library at http://www.dalton.org/libraries/fairrosa is a lovely, very personal Web site. Roxanne Hsu Feldman has a passion for themes, authors, dragons, storytelling, and links to some unusual and interesting related sites.

- The Reading Corner at http://www.carr.lib.md.us/read/ reviews books specifically for children in grades 3–8. Great for author studies, and enough information is given to provide ideas for book talks.

Small Group Literature Studies

In addition to literacy centers, implementing literature study groups keeps students reading and writing while you teach guided reading groups. Literature study groups can be incorporated as part of your rotation or they may be considered an ongoing, long-term project.

Groups are formed based on interest in a specific book and/or by reading ability. Students can work collaboratively or independently on assignments. There may be three or four small groups in your class, each reading a different book. Often, the book is one that the children are reading independently during their silent reading time.

You can oversee the groups by planning a meeting with each group once or twice a week. As your students learn to be more self-directed learners, you will have the time to facilitate and manage these small groups. One technique that works is to have a day of the week when your students visit centers, work on their long-term projects, and meet with their literature study groups. You are then free to circulate and meet with both groups and individuals. Most of these literature studies will require two to four weeks to complete.

Literature study groups build independence. Students in a small group may all be reading the same book, yet choose different activities to complete. Students must adhere to a schedule (when the required number of activities must be completed and when work must be turned in) and be held accountable for the reading and their responses. The use of rubrics sets a standard for expectations.

▸▸ SMALL GROUP LITERATURE STUDIES: A LEARNING STYLES MODEL can be used as a template when you plan and develop your own literature studies. The model is divided into quadrants, each representing a learning style preference (based on studies by Carl Jung). The model was used to create the units for *Fantastic Mr. Fox*, a chapter book, and *Chrysanthemum*, a picture book. The activities in these units are also divided into quadrants which correspond to the learning style quadrants in the model. Students are required to complete two activities in each quadrant and are allowed to choose the remainder of the activities to meet their goals based on the rubric. Extensive research into motivation recommends giving students options; this format provides those options. By requiring activities in each quadrant, students work both in their "comfort zone" and are challenged to stretch themselves as well. A rubric should be provided prior to beginning the literature study.

PAGE 69

Small Group Literature Studies:
A Learning Styles Model

Use this template for planning your own literature studies. Each of the quadrants below describes different kinds of activities which appeal to different learning styles. Creating independent, enthusiastic learners involves finding a way to meet individual styles and preferences. We can't create 30 lessons for every book we use, but we can offer options and choices which provide both a comfort zone and a "stretch." With this unique model for designing literature studies for small groups, students are motivated, accountable, and self-directed. (While collaboration may be an option, individual accountability is required.) The use of rubrics sets standards for goal setting.

#1 Children who are pragmatic and results oriented want to:

Make a list

Write definitions

Fill in the blanks

Keep records

Arrange events in sequence

Follow directions

Demonstrate

Find facts

Note details

Recall information

Make something practical

#2 Children who are empathic and interpersonally oriented want to:

Discuss preferences

Relate personal experiences

Relate personal feelings

Prioritize as to personal importance

Give advantages and disadvantages

Role play

Write in journals

Write poems

Give oral reports

Work cooperatively

#3 Children who are planners and logical thinkers want to:

Compare and contrast

Prove

Evaluate

Ask questions

Write essays

Discuss cause and effect

Explain

Create a logical progression

Design an experiment

Predict consequences

Debate

Summarize

Prioritize based on logic

Categorize

#4 Children who are creative and original want to:

Use imagination

Generate ideas

Find patterns

Dramatize

Illustrate

Design

Predict

Offer many solutions

Produce innovative responses

See possibilities

Use metaphors

Draw

Keep the Rest of the Class Reading and Writing ... While You Teach Small Groups   Scholastic Professional Books

Name: _____

Chrysanthemum

by Kevin Henkes

Directions: Highlight each activity as you work on it. Check off each activity when it is completed. Refer to the rubric before you begin. Do at least two activities in each quadrant and a minimum of 12 activities to receive a 4 on your rubric. Title each page with the task you have chosen. Answer all questions in complete sentences. You may use both sides of the paper and include answers to more than one question on each page. Keep your work in a folder with this page attached to the cover.

☐ Write five mean things that Victoria said to Chrysanthemum. Use quotation marks.

☐ List the names of six other flowers that Mrs. Twinkle might have chosen for her baby.

☐ What were three things Chrysanthemum's parents did to try to make her feel better?

☐ Tell what happened to Victoria at the end of the story.

☐ Tell the story of how you got your name.

☐ Why do you think her parents named her Chrysanthemum? Think of four reasons.

☐ What would you have done if you had been Chrysanthemum and someone had made fun of your name?

☐ What do your mom or dad do to try to make you feel happy when you are sad? Does it help? Why?

☐ What is the lesson Victoria learned in this story?

☐ What is the lesson Chrysanthemum learned in this story?

☐ Make up five questions you would ask Victoria.

☐ How did Chrysanthemum learn to love her name again?

☐ Why do you think Chrysanthemum should be allowed to change her name?

☐ Write an acrostic name poem for Chrysanthemum. Use each letter of her name to tell something about her.

☐ Tell three ways that this story would have been different if Chrysanthemum's name had been Rose.

☐ Create a birth announcement for Mrs. Twinkle's new baby.

☐ Tell four ways this story is like *Chester's Way* (also by Kevin Henkes).

☐ Research chrysanthemums (the flower) and write a short paragraph telling how they are like the main character.

Name: _____

Fantastic Mr. Fox

by Roald Dahl

Directions: Highlight each activity as you work on it. Check off each activity when it is completed. Refer to the rubric before you begin. Do at least two activities in each quadrant and a minimum of 12 activities to receive a 4 on your rubric. Title each page with the task you have chosen. Answer all questions in complete sentences. You may use both sides of the paper and include answers to more than one question on each page. Keep your work in a folder with this page attached to the cover.

☐ When you have finished reading half the book (through chapter nine), write down 10 important events in the order that they happened.

☐ After you have finished the book, think about the factual information you have learned. Write five sentences telling factual, not fictional, information.

☐ Make a list of 15 nouns from the story.

☐ Make a list of 15 adjectives from the story.

☐ Find 10 contractions and tell what each one means.

☐ Why did you feel sorry for the fox even though he was a thief?

☐ Write three pyramid poems, one describing each of the farmers.

☐ If you had to be one of the farmers, which would you rather be and why? (Give at least three reasons.)

☐ Which chapter did you like the most? Why? Give at least three reasons in paragraph form.

☐ Describe the importance of each of the other animals in the story.

☐ Write a two or three sentence summary of each chapter. Skip lines between each summary.

☐ Compare yourself to Mr. Fox. Include several personality traits in your comparison.

☐ If you were Mr. Fox and had to go to court and argue that you had a right to the food you took, what reasons would you give? (Explain in at least six sentences.)

☐ If Boggis, Bunce, and Bean were to go to court and argue that Mr. Fox had no right to the food he took, what reasons would they give? (Explain in at least six sentences.)

☐ Design a storehouse for Mr. Fox. Include shelves and cupboards, and create an inventory.

☐ Create a picture of the underground village that all the animals would live in together. Draw connecting tunnels and show the distance between the animals' homes in feet (one inch = one foot).

☐ Create a one-page sequel to the story, telling what happened after the farmers had waited and waited.

☐ Give 10 reasons why Mr. Fox is considered a "fantastic" fox.

☐ Prepare a script, and dramatize a scene from the story with a friend.

Rubric for Literature Studies

Title: _____

4 _____ **or more activities were completed.**

All spelling has been proofread and corrected.

All pages are in order.

There is an excellent Table of Contents.

There is an excellent and well-illustrated title page.

All work is neatly done.

3 _____ **or more activities were completed.**

Most spelling is proofread and corrected.

All pages are in order

There is a complete Table of Contents

There is an illustrated title page

Most work is neatly done.

2 _____ **or more activities were completed.**

Some spelling is proofread and corrected.

Most pages are in order.

The Table of Contents is incomplete.

The title page shows little effort.

Some work is neatly done.

1 _____ **or more activities were completed.**

Most spelling has not been proofread or corrected.

Many pages missing or out of order

The title page is missing or poorly done.

The Table of Contents is missing or incomplete.

Little effort has been made to turn in neat work.

....

Teacher Instructions: This rubric may be adapted for use when assessing work done during small-group literature studies. Students should have the rubric to refer to, as it allows them to set goals and work toward a specific standard. Also, save high-quality student examples to provide a model for future students. Remember: You may adapt the number of activities which must be completed for each unit so that it is a fit for your grade level and your classroom.

Keep the Rest of the Class Reading and Writing ... While You Teach Small Groups Scholastic Professional Books

More Small Group Literacy-Focused Activities

>> **FABLES** continues the concept of literature study groups with activities based on learning styles. Instead of focusing on one title, however, students are sent to the library (or to your classroom collection of books) to investigate a variety of fables. They are encouraged to work together on these assignments even though they may not be reading the same books. Fables can be shared quite easily. Since two activities from each quadrant are required, you may want to adapt the rubric on page 72.

>> **PROVERBS FROM AROUND THE WORLD** explains what proverbs are and lists several examples.

>> **PROVERBIAL WISDOM** is a companion sheet to proverbs that lists a variety of tasks from which students are to choose. Because discussion will generate thinking, this is an ideal activity for students to work on together.

>> **SETTING THE TABLEAU** is wonderful for a small group, literacy-focused activity. It requires no activity pages, just some initial teacher direction. A tableau (short for *tableau vivant*) is a living picture, a depiction of a scene presented on a stage by motionless participants. The scene should be one from a literature selection, something that all in the group have read, such as the scene in *The BFG* when the BFG, Sophie, and the Queen are having breakfast together.

Each tableau should have no more than four or five participants, each with a speaking part that may be written and rehearsed but is more of a commentary on a situation than memorized lines. Scripts should not be read. Participants should talk directly to the audience, assuming the role of a character. The tableau is practiced during the center rotation time.

A narrator introduces the tableau to the audience, setting the scene; for instance, "Sophie explained to the Queen why they were there, and the Queen was absolutely shocked that the giants were eating her subjects." While the narrator is introducing the tableau, the participants should remain as still as statues, but not in an unnatural stance. One at a time, each member of the tableau will "unfreeze" from the scene and:

1. Tell who he is
2. Describe his part in the scene
3. Talk about how he feels about what is going on.

The "unfrozen" speaker should talk for two or three minutes and may even answer questions from the audience. Then the speaker should again assume the frozen position in the tableau, and the next character should "unfreeze" to speak. The narrator may wish to make "closing" remarks.

Name: _____

Fables

Directions: For this activity, you are to read several fables. Find the section in your library where books of fables are shelved. Choose one or two fable collections that look interesting to you. You don't have to read the entire book, but you do have to read 10 different fables. Highlight each activity as you work on it. You must do two activities from each quadrant. Check each one off when it is completed. You may work with friends, even if you are reading fables from different books.

☐ Read 10 fables and list their titles alphabetically.

☐ List all the smart characters and all the foolish characters in all 10 fables.

☐ Write out the morals for each of the fables.

☐ Find 10 words in the fables whose meanings you do not know, and define them.

☐ Tell which fable you liked best and give at least four reasons why you liked it. Use complete sentences and write in paragraph format.

☐ Work with a friend, and write any fable in play format. Perform it for the class.

☐ Give at least three reasons why you think fables could teach good behavior.

☐ Write a telephone poem about one of the fables.

☐ Explain each of the morals in your own words.

☐ Which fable do you think teaches the most important lesson? Why do you think it is the most important?

☐ How could you put the 10 fables into categories? Can they be grouped by their morals? Can they be grouped by the characters or the setting? Are some funny and some serious? Think of a way to categorize them.

☐ Choose any two fables and explain their similarities and differences.

☐ Create your own morals for four of the fables.

☐ Write a fable of your own with a moral.

☐ What are three things that you've noticed that most fables have in common?

☐ Illustrate a scene from one of the fables. Title the scene with the fable's title.

☐ What kind of behaviors today should have fables written about them? List at least five behaviors that deserve a fable.

Name: _____

Proverbs From Around the World

If you have ever had someone say to you, "Don't cry over spilled milk," or comment, "Easy come, easy go," then you have received advice in the form of a proverb. Proverbs are simply short bits of wisdom that people all over the world have used for thousands of years. Proverbs offer advice and explanations on how we ought to feel about things that happen to us. They don't lecture or preach long sermons; they sum up in a few well-chosen words what experience has taught. People of different cultures, living thousands of miles apart, often have very similar proverbs, because each proverb is about a problem that occurs frequently in the lives of all human beings. Proverbs are a form of folklore that is essentially universal. Think about these proverbs:

He who rides the tiger finds it difficult to dismount.

He who stands with his feet on two ships will be drowned.

If you want to go fast, go the old road.

Little by little grow the bananas.

Two captains sink the ship.

Ice three feet thick isn't frozen in a day.

If you climb up a tree, you must climb down that same tree.

Eggs must not quarrel with stones.

By trying often, the monkey learns to jump from the tree.

Palm nuts do not ripen while you stand under the tree.

Many a good man is found under a shabby hat.

A stone in the water doesn't comprehend how parched the hill is.

Young gambler, old beggar.

The man who is carried on another's back does not appreciate how far off the town is.

A horse that arrives early gets good drinking water.

Keep the Rest of the Class Reading and Writing ... While You Teach Small Groups   Scholastic Professional Books

Proverbial Wisdom

Directions: Use the page PROVERBS FROM AROUND THE WORLD for this activity. Complete six or more of the options below. As you finish each task, check it off and put your answer page in a folder with the rest of this work. Remember to answer in complete sentences and to title each answer (e.g., Five of the Proverbs That Make the Most Sense to Me).

☐ Highlight five of the proverbs that make the most sense to you. Explain each one.

☐ Circle five of the proverbs that don't make any sense to you. Discuss them with a friend, and write down what you think each one means.

☐ Which proverb do you think gives the best advice? Write a paragraph explaining why it is useful.

☐ Find clues in six of the proverbs that tell you where they might have originated. Name the countries that might be possibilities.

☐ Write an imaginative story to explain the origin of one of the proverbs.

☐ Describe an event in your life when one of the proverbs would have been appropriate.

☐ Choose a proverb that might have been important to an explorer. Tell why.

☐ Choose a proverb that might have been important to an inventor. Tell why.

☐ Choose a proverb that you think would be valuable to someone you know. Explain how.

☐ Create a one-page readers' theater script using two or three of the proverbs.

☐ Which proverb is your mom or dad most likely to say to you? Would you agree?

☐ What proverb would you be most likely to say to your mom or dad? What would their response be?

☐ Do you know any other proverbs? Find five more proverbs and write them down.

Challenge Centers and Independent Study Projects

The activities in this chapter offer your students many opportunities to be self-directed learners when confronted with an intellectual challenge. These ideas and activities encourage critical thinking. The ready-to-use pages have a dual purpose. They may, of course, be used "as is," but they were also designed to adapt to your specific curriculum and grade level.

▸▸ **BOOK REPORT MENU** provides a "menu" of choices following the independent reading of a book. This format can be used with chapter books as well as picture books.

▸▸ **CHECK FOUR: CREATE YOUR OWN BOOK REPORT** again offers choices. Students choose any four questions to answer following the independent reading of a book. It is a variation on the usual book report and may be used as an assessment as well. The open-ended questioning model encourages higher-level thinking in student responses.

▸▸ **THE READING RESPONSE RUBRIC** adds a bit of humor to the serious business of assessment. Since students need to know what the standards are for grading, rubrics should be given to students when assignments are made. Use this all-purpose rubric for assessing writing related to reading.

▸▸ **COMEDY, CATASTROPHE, AND COMEUPPANCE** is an independent study designed to encourage a closer look at some of the delightful devices employed by author Roald Dahl. Consider an author study, using the categories on this sheet, with a small group reading different Dahl books.

▸▸ **THE SEVEN WONDERS OF THE ANCIENT WORLD"** and its accompanying **WORKSHEET** are provided to reinforce question asking. Comprehension is increased when students are required to formulate questions about their reading. This model can be used across the curriculum when factual knowledge is the focus.

▸▸ **ADD ADJECTIVES TO YOUR VOCABULARY** is a multipurpose list. For this assignment, students are to identify feelings experienced by a book's main character, but the list may be used in many other ways. Consider posting it as a special word wall for children to reference when writing, or add the words gradually to weekly spelling assignments.

PAGE 87 ▸▸ **SHOWING, NOT TELLING: USING WORDS TO CREATE PICTURES** also focuses on words—words that authors use to help readers visualize a scene. This activity builds awareness of the author's craft. Students will search out or write their own "showing" sentences.

PAGE 88 ▸▸ **PADDLE-TO-THE-SEA** is a format for creating thematic units of study. This one is designed as a type of contract for an individual student, but the ideas can be excerpted and used effectively as you read aloud from this book. Students in a literature study group can work through assignments collaboratively if multiple copies of the book are available.

PAGE 89 ▸▸ **EYEWITNESS JUNIORS: AMAZING FLYING MACHINES** provides a format for building research skills by asking students to use the index to find evidence to support or refute statements. Use the index of any book to teach and reinforce research skills. Teach students that a comma follows the word *yes* or *no* when answering questions to reinforce that grammatical rule.

PAGE 90 ▸▸ The **INDEPENDENT RESEARCH PROJECT** is a step-by-step guide for creating written and oral reports and special projects. It is designed for students who are at different levels of independence. It can also be used as a whole-class directed lesson for first-time researchers. The use of a web for research-based note taking and as the basis for writing paragraphs is stressed. Below is a model of this web. Guided practice in its use should precede independent work.

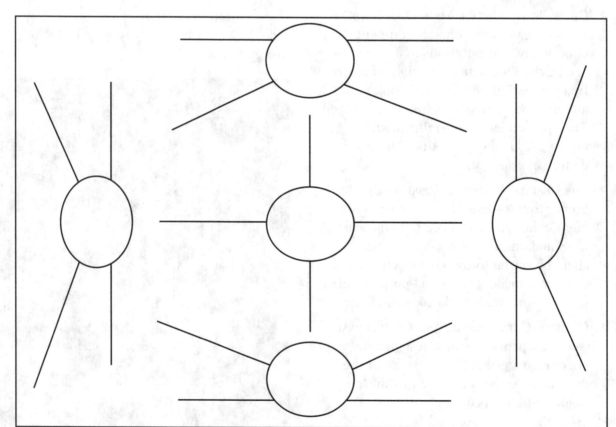

Sample of a research project web

Book Report Menu

Choose one item from each column

What three questions would you ask the author if he or she were here?	What was the setting? How did the author tell you about the setting?	How did the cover art prepare you for the story? Describe it. Was the illustration accurate?	If you were able to meet one of the characters, whom would you choose and what would you talk about?
What kinds of illustrations are used in your book? How did they help tell the story? Would you have changed any of them?	What did you think was the most important part of the story? What happened, and why was it important?	If you were the author, would you have ended the story the same way or would you end it differently? How would you end it? Why?	How important was the title? Would you change it? What title would you give it? Why?
Find and list at least five words or phrases you would like to add to your personal vocabulary. Define any that you do not know.	What were the surprises in this story? Tell about two or three instances where you could not have predicted what happened.	Find three examples of "telling" sentences and three examples of "showing" paragraphs. Copy them and comment on the differences.	What was the main problem of the story? How was it solved?
Some books have more than one problem. Tell about others that were in your book.	Draw a picture of the most interesting part of your book. Caption the picture with two or three sentences explaining the scene you've pictured.	Find a total of at least 10 examples of any of the following: personification, alliteration, metaphors, similes, onomatopoeia, or idioms.	Collect 10 or 15 sesquipedalian words. List them, look them up, and then tell which one you like best.

Attach this menu to your answer sheet. All answers must be proofread and written in complete sentences. The best answers for most of the questions will be about one paragraph in length. You should have four paragraphs when you have finished.

Keep the Rest of the Class Reading and Writing ... While You Teach Small Groups Scholastic Professional Books

Check Four:
Create Your Own Book Report

Name: _____ **Date:** _____

Book Title: _____

Author: _____

Check four questions that you would like to answer about your book. Answer each question in paragraph form and staple this page to your answer page.

☐ Who is your favorite character? Why?

☐ Whom do you know who is like that character?

☐ Is there a scene from the book you can picture in your mind? Describe it.

☐ What were you thinking about when the story ended?

☐ If you had been there, what would you have done?

☐ What didn't you understand?

☐ What questions would you like to ask the author?

☐ In your opinion, what was the most important event in the story?

☐ What clues in the story told you how it was going to end?

☐ When were you surprised?

☐ What was hard for you to believe?

☐ In what ways was this book similar to another that you've read?

Reading Response Rubric

4 ☐ Each answer is written in a complete sentence.
☐ Answers are thoughtful and well written.
☐ Spelling has been proofread and corrected.
☐ Special directions have been followed (example: each sentence must have an adjective).
☐ There are fewer than two errors in punctuation and capitalization
☐ This paper was written in cursive.
☐ The project is neat and well organized.

(The teacher wants to put it on the bulletin board in the office so everyone can see it.)

3 ☐ Each answer is written in a complete sentence.
☐ Most answers are thoughtful and well written.
☐ Most spelling has been proofread and corrected.
☐ Special directions have been followed.
☐ There are no more than four errors in punctuation and capitalization.
☐ This paper was written in cursive.
☐ The project is fairly neat and well organized.

(The teacher wants to put it on the bulletin board in the room so that the class can see it.)

2 ☐ Some answers are not written in complete sentences.
☐ Some answers are not thoughtful or well written.
☐ Some spelling has been corrected.
☐ Special directions are followed some of the time.
☐ There are many punctuation and capitalization errors.
☐ This paper was written in cursive.
☐ The project is not very neat or well organized

(You want to hide this paper. You are thinking about doing it over.)

1 ☐ Answers are not in complete sentences.
☐ Answers show little thought.
☐ There are numerous spelling errors.
☐ Special directions have not been followed.
☐ There are many punctuation and capitalization errors.
☐ This paper was written in cursive.
☐ The project is messy with poor organization.

(You do hide the paper and you do start over.)

Many thanks to Pat Ward and Cathy Bullock for sharing this humorous and useful rubric.

Name: _____

Comedy, Catastrophe, and Comeuppance

Roald Dahl's books are full of humorous events, horrible happenings, and happy endings. The protagonists (the good guys) receive their rewards, and the antagonists (the bad guys) get their comeuppance. Choose one of these books to read and then discuss the comedy, catastrophes, and comeuppance.

- *The BFG*
- *The Magic Finger*
- *Danny, The Champion of the World*
- *Matilda*
- *Fantastic Mr. Fox*

The Comedy (Tell about some of the humor.)

Catastrophes (Tell about some of the horrible happenings.)

Comeuppance (What happened to the "bad guys" at the end?)

The Seven Wonders of the Ancient World

If you had been a tourist in ancient Greece or Rome a few thousand years ago, you might have been told to travel to each of the following destinations in order to see what were then considered extraordinary works of art and architecture. These structures were regarded with awe primarily because of their huge size. Today, only the Pyramids of Egypt still stand.

The Pyramids of Egypt at Giza, built between 2700 and 1000 BC, are the oldest of the seven wonders and were built as burial places for Egyptian rulers. These tombs had square bases and four triangular sides and were built with blocks of stone, each weighing more than two tons. The largest pyramid, the Khufu Pyramid, covers an area of 13 acres. There were no cranes or heavy building equipment so all construction was done by teams of men working together.

The Hanging Gardens of Babylon were built by King Nebuchadnezzar II in 562 BC for his favorite wife, Amytis. In actuality, the gardens didn't really hang, but were a series of planted terraces progressing upward in a mountain-like structure. Flowers, trees, and avenues of palms were planted in these terraces. They were irrigated by water pumped to fountains from the Euphrates River. They were easily visible from the city of Babylon and existed for over two hundred years.

The Statue of Zeus, king of the Greek gods, was built in the middle of the 5th century BC by the sculptor Phidias. The 40-foot sculpture of ivory and gold was the central feature of the Temple of Zeus at Olympia, Greece. The statue, which showed Zeus seated on his throne, was struck by lightning and destroyed. It is only from ancient coins that we have an idea what this majestic statue must have looked like.

The Temple of Artemis, at Ephesus in Greece, was built to honor the Greek goddess of nature, Artemis, called Diana by the Romans. It was begun in 541 BC and said to have taken 220 years to complete after contributions were made from all the cities of Asia. The temple was set on fire and destroyed by the Goths in 262 A.D.

The Mausoleum at Halicarnassus got its name from King Mausolus whose wife, Artemisia, had Greek architects build this tomb in his memory in 352 B.C. On top of its huge rectangular base stood 36 columns and 36 statues, all of which held a pyramid-shaped roof. At the top of that roof was a four-horse chariot in which were statues of the king and queen. This structure was so famous that all monumental tombs today are known as mausoleums. In 1402, the Mausoleum was destroyed so that the stone could be used to build a castle for the Knights of Saint John.

The Colossus of Rhodes was a giant bronze statue representing the Greek sun god Helios and was supposed to be over 100 feet high. It was erected about 280 B.C. to guard the entrance to the harbor at Rhodes and to commemorate the successful defense of Rhodes against its enemies. It stood guard for approximately 55 years, at which time it was toppled by an earthquake.

The Tower of Pharos was a great lighthouse built on the island of Pharos, at Alexandria, Egypt. Built in 285 BC, during the reign of Ptolemy, it guided ships into the harbor for more than a thousand years. The lighthouse was over 500 hundred feet high and made of white marble. The light, created by a mirror which reflected a fire at the top of its stone tower, could be seen from a distance of 42 miles. Like the Colossus of Rhodes, an earthquake destroyed the Tower of Pharos.

Keep the Rest of the Class Reading and Writing ... While You Teach Small Groups   Scholastic Professional Books

Name: _____

The Seven Wonders of the Ancient World

Directions: Each paragraph on this page has a great deal of factual information. After carefully reading each paragraph, create three questions based on facts presented in the paragraph.

	Question	Question	Question
Paragraph 2			
Paragraph 3			
Paragraph 4			
Paragraph 5			
Paragraph 6			
Paragraph 7			
Paragraph 8			

Name: _____

Add Adjectives to Your Vocabulary

These adjectives describe how someone feels. Write the name of the main character in the book you are reading next to at least 10 of these adjectives when he or she demonstrates that feeling. Use the dictionary to confirm your understanding of the word before you assign the adjective.

Title of Book _____

addled	dejected
agitated	despondent
afraid	detached
ambivalent	determined
annoyed	discouraged
antagonistic	disgusted
anxious	ecstatic
apprehensive	elated
baffled	embarrassed
belligerent	enthusiastic
bewildered	euphoric
bored	exasperated
calm	excited
cautious	exuberant
confident	foolish
confused	fortunate
connected	frantic
curious	frustrated

furious	mystified
grateful	nervous
hopeful	objective
hostile	open-minded
humiliated	optimistic
hurried	overwhelmed
hungry	perplexed
introspective	preoccupied
helpless	puzzled
inadequate	resentful
insecure	scared
interested	surprised
intrigued	sympathetic
intuitive	tense
involved	terrific
irate	thrilled
irritated	tranquil
jittery	troubled
jolly	uncomfortable
jubilant	undecided
lightheaded	uneasy
lucky	uninterested
mischievous	vexed
mixed-up	wonderful

Name: _____

Showing, Not Telling: Using Words to Create Pictures

Directions: Authors make reading more fun by helping us visualize what is happening. Instead of saying *Tom was scared,* a writer might say: *His hair stood on end...he felt hot and cold at the same time...he rubbed his hands together to stay warm, then fanned himself to stay cool.* On the left side of this table is a word that "tells" a feeling. On the right side of the table, describe behavior that would demonstrate or show that feeling. You can find examples in books or you can write your own.

Fear	*Example:* "Beads of perspiration covered his forehead, his pulse was pounding, he looked back over his shoulder. He kept moving."
Curiosity	
Surprise	
Disgust	
Determination	
Confusion	
Elation	
Embarrassment	
Enthusiasm	

Paddle-to-the-Sea

by Holling Clancy Holling

An Independent Study Project

SCIENCE

- In your own words, from the information in Chapter 2, explain why the boy was so sure that Paddle would make it to the sea. (Conduct a water drops experiment to see which size drop travels fastest on a slant and whether the angle of the slant makes a difference.)

- Look carefully at the diagram of the canal lock in Chapter 17. Copy the drawings and use the text to help you caption your drawing with an explanation of how canals work. Use the encyclopedia (look up "canal") for an in-depth explanation and examples.

- What weather and water conditions affected Paddle's travels? (Be sure to include currents.)

SOCIAL STUDIES

- Map Paddle's travels chapter by chapter. (The map at the end of the book is a big help!)

- Keep a timeline of the major events throughout the story as Paddle goes to the sea.

- Chapter 8 describes "the largest lake in the world." Tell which lake it is and several reasons why it is distinctive.

- Learn the names of all the Great Lakes.

LANGUAGE ARTS

- There are vocabulary words that need to be defined. Define as you go on an "as needed" basis, but be sure to include: rudder, ballast, portaging, dry dock, and piling.

- The author uses many similes and metaphors to describe Paddle's adventures. Locate and list at least 10 similes and metaphors. Tell which one is your favorite and why.

- Create a Venn diagram to compare and contrast the video and the book. Expand upon the diagrams to write an opinion of which was "best."

- Write the names of at least 20 places that Paddle visited. Be sure to capitalize these proper nouns.

MATH CONCEPTS

- Compare the length of the Sault Ste. Marie Canal in Canada to the Suez Canal and the Panama Canal.

- Compute the mileage that Paddle traveled.

RELATED ARTS

- Sketch Lake Superior using the drawings in Chapter 8 as a guide.

- Learn the words to the traditional song, "The Erie Canal."

- Paddle was exactly one foot long. Draw him to scale.

Keep the Rest of the Class Reading and Writing ... While You Teach Small Groups   Scholastic Professional Books

Eyewitness Juniors: Amazing Flying Machines

by Robin Kerrod

Finding Evidence Using the Index

Use the index to find evidence to support or refute the statements below. Write each sentence in the space provided. Begin your sentence with the word *Yes* or *No*, and don't forget to follow *Yes* or *No* with a comma.

Alcock and Brown made the first nonstop crossing of the Atlantic in 26 hours in 1919.

Chuck Yeager named the plane in which he broke the sound barrier after his wife.

The Montgolfier brothers believed that the warm air would lift their cold air balloon.

The secret of the helicopter is that its rotor blades have two important functions.

The Goodyear Blimp, which is still being used today, was created by Count Ferdinand von Zeppelin.

The Concorde and the Lockheed Electra are the only two modern airliners flying at supersonic speed.

Independent Research Project

Name: _____

Research Topic: _____

Project Title: _____ **Date due:** _____

Your research project must be submitted in a folder with an illustrated cover and will include:

☐ A TITLE PAGE (with project title, an illustration, and your name as author)

☐ NOTE-TAKING WEB

A web is a collection of clusters. A cluster is a circle with lines, or spokes, extending from it. Inside the circle is a topic. At the end of the spokes are facts related to the topic. You will need five clusters for your web. Each cluster will have a different subtopic in it. For instance, if you were researching an animal, subtopics might include physical appearance, diet, habitat, importance to the ecosystem, and caring for young. You may adjust or add subtopics as you research. You may add spokes as you need to. Your web of notes should be included in your folder after the bibliography.

☐ A FIVE- OR SIX-PARAGRAPH REPORT

Use the information in your web to create a report summarizing your findings about the topic you researched.

Each cluster will have the facts you will need to write a paragraph about the subtopic. Each subtopic should be represented by a paragraph in your report. Write an interesting topic sentence for each paragraph. If you have enough "extra" information, add a paragraph to incorporate other interesting facts uncovered in your research as well as any opinions you have about your topic. Write a powerful closing sentence in your last paragraph.

☐ BIBLIOGRAPHY

You must use at two or three sources (books or the encyclopedia) of information. Title a page "Bibliography" and list the books you used for your report. The bibliography must be in alphabetical order by author's last name. The format for a bibliography is: author's last name, author's first name, a period; book title (underlined), a period; the place it was published, a colon; the name of the publisher, a comma; the date of publication, and a period. See the sample below:

Fredericks, Anthony D. <u>Weird Walkers</u>. Wisconsin: NorthWord Press, Inc., 1996.

If you use an encyclopedia, put it in alphabetically this way:

World Book Encyclopedia. Volume 3. Pages 75-82. 1987.

☐ A SPECIAL PROJECT

This is where you get to use your imagination. You can make a poster, a mural, a diorama, a slide show, or a video about your topic. You may also write a pyramid poem, a telephone poem, or a two-word poem or combine any of these with artwork.

☐ ORAL REPORT

You might share your information with the class as an oral report. The presentation of information about your topic should be from two to four minutes in length. You should practice your report and know your topic so well that you do not have to refer to notes.

You will be graded on content (the information you have), spelling, cursive (and overall neatness), and mechanics (punctuation, indenting paragraphs, and use of capital letters when needed). Have a parent or other adult proofread your report.

☐ This research report was proofread.

_____   _____
Adult Signature   Date

Please check off each item above when you have finished it. Include this sheet in your folder.

Genre Studies

Centers are an ideal way to introduce the concept of genres. Use picture books, chapter books, or a combination of the two, but concentrate on one genre at a time. You can spend eight to 10 weeks pursuing genre studies, or you can space these activities throughout the year. The different genre centers are also "stand-alones," should you prefer to use them as unrelated to a larger theme-type study.

PAGE
94

▸▸ GENRE JOURNEY is the introductory activity designed to present the idea of genres and build interest in reading different kinds of books. Asking students to provide a definition for each genre is a variation of an anticipation guide. They are encouraged to put a question mark if they don't know the definition and invited to write it if they do (or think they do). As your students have different experiences with the varied genres, have them add to their initial definitions. At the end of the study, the same sheet can be used as an assessment.

PAGE
95

▸▸ PICTURE THE POSSIBILITIES presents a genre "menu." Activities vary from genre to genre, and all related work may be kept in a folder with this page as the cover. If you focus on each genre for two to three weeks, it provides time to read aloud from a book of the same genre.

PAGE
96

▸▸ The BIOGRAPHY WEB will have the name of the subject in the center of the web. The spokes extend out to four different clusters or subtopics: Early Years, Significant Events, Character Traits, and Contributions. Spokes extend from each of the subtopics for note taking. As facts are discovered, spokes may be added. Each cluster or subtopic of the completed web forms the basis for a paragraph, so

the writing of a four-paragraph biography can be encouraged.

PAGE
97

▸▸ BIOGRAPHY: A GENRE INVESTIGATION is far more challenging and requires a great deal more investigation than the biography web. Directions and tasks are given for creating a six-paragraph biography report.

PAGE
98

▸▸ MY GREAT-AUNT ARIZONA is a picture book biography. The activity page's "True-False" format requires students to go to the book for answers. This activity builds comprehension, is an effective partner center, and it may be used across genres. There is a blank form for you to use with other picture books. Ask your students to create their own "true-false" questions upon finishing a book.

PAGE
100

▸▸ A BRIEF BIOGRAPHY BIBLIOGRAPHY is provided because it will make your job easier and it is better to send students to the library with specific titles and authors.

PAGE
101

▸▸ POETRY MENU requires a trip to the library to bring a number of anthologies into your classroom (be sure to include some Jack Prelutsky).

PAGE
102

▸▸ SCIENCE FICTION: FUTURISTIC TECHNOLOGY, INTERGALACTIC TRAVEL, AND ALIEN CIVILIZATIONS provides a wealth of science fiction authors and book titles. The STUDENT ASSIGNMENT SHEET details the related work. Using science fiction as an expanded theme, this study could be contrasted with another genre, also done as an expanded theme.

PAGE
104

▸▸ Students should read a mystery by one of the AUTHORS WHO WRITE MYSTERIES and create their own web. The web's clusters should include "Suspenseful Events" and "Clues." Since these authors write books in other genres, make sure that your students are choosing mystery books.

PAGE 105

➤➤ ADVENTURE ACTIVITIES details the motifs that must be present for a story to be an adventure. An unfamiliar situation, danger, the use of one's wits, courage, and a return to safety are all part of the equation. (Aha! *The Wizard of Oz*, then, must be a fantasy adventure!)

PAGE 106

➤➤ AUTHORS' AUTOBIOGRAPHIES lists recent books of this genre. Students are asked to create a cluster of facts about the author.

PAGE 107

➤➤ HUMOR IN LITERATURE: RIB TICKLERS AND FUNNY BONES describes some of the elements of humorous writing. Remember not to overanalyze; funny quickly becomes unfunny. The basics of paragraph writing are reinforced here with the humorous element used as the topic sentence and examples as supporting sentences. FUNNY BOOKS is a table that can be used as a resource for authors and titles, but also may be the basis for a lengthier genre study.

PAGE 109

➤➤ What happens in fantasies cannot possibly happen in real life. Animals talk and behave as people do, worlds are invented, and story characters can travel through time, become invisible, see ghosts, and weave magic spells. TIME TRAVEL: A DIFFERENT KIND OF JOURNEY explains the motifs that make this form of fantasy so unique. Book titles and author examples are provided, and TIME TRAVEL: A WEEKLY READING LOG focuses on those motifs.

PAGE 111

➤➤ HAPPILY EVER AFTER HEADLINES continues the fantasy genre with a fairy tale activity. Using this model headlines can be written for all story genres.

PAGE 112

➤➤ *REDWALL: A CHOICE MENU* is deliberately aimed at Brian Jacques fans (and potential fans). This fabulous fantasy series has several books now and is ideal for grades four and above for independent reading. If you choose to use this book as a readaloud to introduce the genre or the series, excerpt some of the activities for the whole class.

➤➤ Use a readaloud, either a chapter book or a picture book, to introduce each new genre. Call attention to the characteristics that distinguish the genre. Some ideas for readalouds are:

BIOGRAPHY:
What's the Big Idea, Ben Franklin?
by Jean Fritz

SCIENCE FICTION:
The Green Book
by Jill Paton Walsh

ADVENTURE:
Number the Stars
by Lois Lowry

HUMOR:
Frindle by Andrew Clements
The BFG by Roald Dahl
Wayside School Is Falling Down
By Louis Sacher

POETRY:
Any of the poetry collections of Jack Prelutsky, Douglas Florian, and many others

MYSTERY:
The Headless Cupid by Mary Downing Hahn

AUTOBIOGRAPHY:
Bill Peet, An Autobiography

FANTASY:
Tuck Everlasting
by Natalie Babbitt
Jeremy Thatcher, Dragon Hatcher
by Bruce Coville
Poppy
by Avi

Genre Journey

Each of the words below describes a certain kind of book. What do these descriptions mean? If you know or think you know what you would expect to find in a book of that type, explain it. If you're not sure, put a question mark in the ? column.

Genre	?	Definition
Biography		
Science Fiction		
Adventure		
Humor		
Poetry		
Mystery		
Autobiography		
Fantasy		

Name: _____ **Date due:** _____

Picture the Possibilities

Do you always read one kind of book? For this project, you will explore all different types of books. These types are called *genres*. When you have chosen a book in one of these genres, you may partner read it with a friend or read it independently. When you have finished reading, there will be a different task required for each genre. Since this project will continue for several weeks, please keep all your work in a folder to turn in on the date this project is due.

Biography

Science Fiction

Adventure

HUMOR

Poetry

MYSTERY

Autobiography

Fantasy

Biography Web

Significant Events in Life

Contributions

Early Years

Character Traits

Name: _____

Biography: A Genre Investigation

Choose someone whose life you would like to research. Answer one question in each quadrant and then choose two other questions to answer—six questions and a minimum of six paragraphs. Each paragraph should be at least four sentences in length. Some answers may require more than one paragraph. The paragraphs should be in an order that makes sense when they are read.

1. Describe your subject's family. What were the parents like? What were their occupations? What were their problems? What was "growing up" like?

2. What was the educational background of your subject? Schools attended? What advantages or disadvantages did this person have in his schooling? What was important during this time?

3. What were some benchmark events? What specific occurrences along the way helped this person become successful?

4. What were your subject's main strengths? What were his or her special talents or skills? How were they developed? How do you think they helped your person become famous?

5. Would you describe this person as a hero? What reasons do you have?

6. What character traits and personality qualities did this person have? Which quality was most helpful? Which character trait was least helpful or a negative influence?

7. Describe a high point in the life of your subject. Explain why this was a "high point" and why it was of great importance.

8. Explain in detail what this person did. What major issues were a concern? What type of work was involved?

9. Did you discover conflicting information about your subject that you think is particularly interesting? Tell about it.

10. What were the consequences of your subject's accomplishments? What proof is there that those accomplishments have made a difference?

11. Tell about one important event in your subject's life that was an obstacle to overcome. Describe how it was overcome and the difference it made.

12. Summarize this person's major accomplishments.

13. Locate a quotation that you think describes the person you researched. Explain why it fits your subject.

Name: _____

My Great-Aunt Arizona

By Gloria Houston

How much do you know about *My Great-Aunt Arizona*?

	TRUE	FALSE
1. She was named Arizona because that's where she was born.	TRUE	FALSE
2. She traveled to many faraway places.	TRUE	FALSE
3. She taught school for 57 years.	TRUE	FALSE
4. The children called her Miz Shoes because she wore high-button shoes.	TRUE	FALSE
5. Arizona liked to read and sing and dance.	TRUE	FALSE
6. Petticoats are pretty white aprons.	TRUE	FALSE
7. Arizona had two brothers.	TRUE	FALSE
8. Jim and Arizona searched for galax and ginseng roots in the creek.	TRUE	FALSE
9. Snow cream is made from the sap of maple trees.	TRUE	FALSE
10. All the children brought Christmas trees to plant.	TRUE	FALSE
11. Arizona and Jim went to a blab school.	TRUE	FALSE
12. A blab school is a school where all the children read their lessons aloud at the same time.	TRUE	FALSE
13. Arizona took her lunch to school and drank cool water out of the drinking fountain.	TRUE	FALSE
14. The Blue Ridge Mountains are near Colorado.	TRUE	FALSE
15. The author admired and loved her Great-Aunt Arizona.	TRUE	FALSE

Name: _____

Book: _____

Author: _____

1.	TRUE	FALSE
2.	TRUE	FALSE
3.	TRUE	FALSE
4.	TRUE	FALSE
5.	TRUE	FALSE
6.	TRUE	FALSE
7.	TRUE	FALSE
8.	TRUE	FALSE
9.	TRUE	FALSE
10.	TRUE	FALSE
11.	TRUE	FALSE
12.	TRUE	FALSE
13.	TRUE	FALSE
14.	TRUE	FALSE
15.	TRUE	FALSE

A Brief Biography Bibliography

Here is a listing of some recent biographies showcasing artists, musicians, sports heroes, and people who have changed history in a number of ways. Most of the books listed are designated for students aged 8–12; a few are included which will appeal to older students and/or more able readers.

One Giant Leap: The Story of Neil Armstrong
Don Brown

Black Whiteness: Admiral Byrd Alone in the Antarctic
Robert Burleigh

Home Run: The Story of Babe Ruth
Robert Burleigh

On the Court with... Lisa Leslie
Matt Christopher

On the Field with...Mia Hamm
Matt Christopher

Carter G. Woodson: Father of African-American History
Robert F. Durder

Nelson Mandela
Reggie Finlayson

Martha Graham: A Dancer's Life
Russell Freedman

Chuck Close, Up Close
Jan Greenberg and Sandra Jordan

Women of Hope: African Americans Who Made a Difference
Joyce Hansen

Mark Twain and the Queens of the Mississippi
Cheryl Harness

How It Was With Dooms: A True Story From Africa
Carol Cawthra Hopcraft and Xan Hopcraft

Madeleine Albright
Megan Howard

Princess Ka'iulani: Hope of a Nation, Heart of a People
Sharon Linnea

Fly, Bessie, Fly
Lynn Joseph

Quincy Jones: Musician, Composer, Producer
Lee Hill Kavanaugh

Sally Ride: A Space Biography
Barbara Kramer

Lives of the Presidents: Fame, Shame (and What the Neighbors Thought)
Kathleen Krull

Arthur Ashe
Caroline Lazo

Dear Benjamin Banneker
Andrea Davis Pinkney

Duke Ellington: The Piano Prince and His Orchestra
Andrea Davis Pinkney

Louisa May Alcott
Amy Ruth

William Bradford: Plymouth's Faithful Pilgrim
Gary Schmidt

Thomas Jefferson: Architect of Democracy
John B. Severance

Behind the Mask: The Life of Elizabeth I
Jane Resh Thomas

Brainstorm! The Stories of Twenty American Kid Inventors
Tom Tucker

My Name Is Georgia: A Portrait
Jeanette Winter

Name: _____

Poetry Menu

Directions: Complete three of the activities on this menu. Attach your work to this sheet before turning it in.

☐ **Read lots of poems. Write down the names of five poets whose poems you really like.**	☐ **Plan to perform or recite one of your favorite poems. You most certainly can do this with a friend.**	☐ **Find an example of a simile, a metaphor, onomatopoeia, and personification in any of the poems you are reading.**
☐ **Find two poems on the same subject by different poets. Write a paragraph about the poem you prefer and why.**	☐ **Turn a poem into a story.**	☐ **Choose a poem you really like and think about some things you notice about it. Write five or more sentences telling things you notice.**
☐ **Find a poem that describes an experience you've had. Write about your experience and how you relate it to the poem.**	☐ **Answer these five questions about any poem:** 1. What was the poem about? 2. Who was the poem about? 3. Where was the poem's setting? 4. Why did this particular poem get your attention? 5. Why was the poem written? (What was the poet's purpose in writing the poem?)	☐ **Write your own poem. Use one of your favorites as a model.**

Name: _____

Science Fiction: Futuristic Technology, Intergalactic Travel, and Alien Civilizations

Directions: Each of the authors below has written at least one science fiction book. Some have written books in other genres. For this study, you will read two science fiction books, each by a different author. To be science fiction, there must be futuristic technology, intergalactic travel, and/or alien civilizations. See the accompanying page for your assignments.

Anne McCaffrey *(Acorna, the Unicorn Girl)*	**Daniel Pinkwater** *(Fat Men From Space)*	**Lois Lowry** *(The Giver)*
Bruce Coville *(Aliens Ate My Homework)*	**Isaac Asimov** *(The Norby Chronicles)*	**Ray Bradbury** *(R Is for Rocket)*
Richard Peck *(The Great Interactive Dream Machine)*	**Mel Gilden** *(Cybercops and Flame Wars)*	**H.M. Hoover** *(The Winds of Mars)*
Edgar Rice Burroughs *(A Princess of Mars series)*	**Arthur C. Clarke** *(Red Sands of Mars)*	**Paula Danziger** *(This Place Has No Atmosphere)*
Tony Abbott *(Cosmic Boy Versus Mezmo Head)*	**Jill Paton Walsh** *(The Green Book)*	**K.A. Applegate** *(The Animorphs series)*
David Cody Weiss *(The Arrival)*	**Jane Yolen** *(Commander Toad series)*	**John Vornholt** *(Startrek: Starfleet Academy series)*
Betsy Byars *(The Computer Nut)*	**Alexander Key** *(The Forgotten Door)*	**Jerry Piasecki** *(Chocolate Rules and the Starship Meatloaf)*

Name: _____

Science Fiction: Futuristic Technology, Intergalactic Travel, and Alien Civilizations

Assignment Sheet

- Science fiction books are shelved in the library according to the author's last name. Create an alphabetized list of the science fiction authors whose names are listed on the table. Use the list to help you locate the two books you will read for this assignment.

- Write the titles and authors of the two books you have chosen:

Title _____

Author _____

Title _____

Author _____

- For each of your books, write one paragraph about the futuristic technology, intergalactic travel, or the alien civilizations depicted.

- For each of your books, create a list of five events that could really happen and five events that could not really happen.

- Discuss the books you read, which you preferred, and your feelings about science fiction.

_____

_____

_____

_____

_____

_____

Name: _____

Authors Who Write Mysteries

Directions: The authors on this list write mysteries. Sometimes they write other kinds of stories as well. Since mysteries are considered fiction, books by these authors will be shelved according to the author's last name. Select a book, but be sure it is a mystery. Read it. When you have finished, design a web about the book that includes clusters for "Suspense" and "Clues." What other clusters will your web need?

- Jean Craighead George
- Laurence Yep
- Lynne Reid Banks
- Mary Downing Hahn
- Elvira Woodruff
- Betsy Byars
- Betty Ren Wright
- John Bellairs

- Matt Christopher
- Donald J. Sobol
- Susan Kimmel Wright
- Gertrude Chandler Warner
- Walter Farley
- Phyllis Reynolds Naylor
- Deborah Howe

- Willo Roberts
- Franklin W. Dixon
- Joan Lowery Nixon
- Parker Hinter
- Linda Lee Maifair
- Natalie Babbitt
- David Adler
- Michael Coleman

These are the books that I'd like to read when I've finished the one for this assignment:

1. _____

2. _____

3. _____

4. _____

5. _____

Name: _____

Adventure Activities

Directions: An adventure usually finds the main character in an unfamiliar situation. There is often danger that requires the characters to be courageous and use their wits and strength to return to safety. Gary Paulsen, Sid Fleischman, and Peg Kehret are three authors who write adventure stories. There are many others. Read an adventure story and choose two of the activities below:

Title _____

Author _____

☐ **Make a timeline of all the major events in the book that make it an adventure.**

☐ **Write a paragraph telling five things you learned while reading the book.**

☐ **Adventure stories are full of conflicts and solutions. Write about three different conflicts and their solutions.**

☐ **Good writers often use unusual and interesting words and expressions. If your book has vocabulary that is worth noting, make a list of at least 15 examples.**

☐ **Discuss the title of the book you read. How do you feel about it? Is it appropriate? Can you think of a better title? How about five better titles? Write down five titles that you think would be better and explain why.**

☐ **How important is the setting of your book? Most adventure stories rely on the setting for the "adventure." If there are a number of locations that influence the action, create a map that shows where events occur. Use a detailed legend that explains the importance of each location.**

☐ **Focus on three different characters in the book you read. Share something that each one of them learned.**

☐ **Make up a multiple choice or a true-false test for your book. Ask 20 questions. Answer your questions on a separate sheet of paper.**

Name: _____

Authors' Autobiographies

Directions: An autobiography is when someone writes about his or her own life. The autobiographies below are all by authors of children's books. Locate one of the books below, read it, and create a cluster about the writer with lots of interesting facts from the book.

Under the Royal Palms:
A Childhood in Cuba
Alma Flor Ada

The Times of My Life: A Memoir
Brent Ashabranner

The Moon and I
Betsy Byars

On the Bus With Joanna Cole
Joanna Cole and Wendy Saul

Dreams and Wishes
Susan Cooper

Bigmama's
Donald Crews

Boy: Tales of Childhood
Roald Dahl

Tom
Tomie dePaola

The Abracadabra Kid: A Writer's Life
Sid Fleischman

Homesick: My Own Story
Jean Fritz

The Tarantula in My Purse
and 172 Other Wild Pets
Jean Craighead George

A Three-Generation Memoir
Eloise Greenfield and Lessie Little

I Was a Teenage Professional Wrestler
Ted Lewin

Little by Little
Jean Little

Looking Back: A Book of Memories
Lois Lowry

In Flight With David McPhail
David McPhail

Woodsong
Gary Paulsen

Bill Peet: An Autobiography
Bill Peet

My Ol' Man
Patricia Polacco

Oddballs
William Sleator

Knots in My Yo-yo String: The
Autobiography of a Kid
Jerry Spinelli

When I Was Nine
James Stevenson

Humor in Literature:
Rib Ticklers and Funny Bones

Humor can come from:

• **Wacky characters**

• **Characters who get themselves in strange situations**

• **Words that create funny pictures in your mind**

• **Great dialogue**

• **Word play**

• **Surprises**

• **Illustrations**

• **Gross and yucky stuff**

• **Silliness**

Sometimes what 's funny to us is just a matter of "getting" the joke. That's why what's funny to one person may not be funny to another. On the next page there is a grid with lots of funny books. The ones shown are examples of books you might read, but you can read any humorous book by the authors named (or any humorous book by an author who is not named). Remember, just because a book is humorous doesn't mean the whole book is funny. It may just have some funny parts. Keep your eyes open for the funny parts!

Read one of the books. What made it funny? Use two or three of the ideas above and give examples to show what you mean (For instance: *The book I chose was really silly. George and Harold hypnotized their principal and he thought he was a superhero named Captain Underpants!*) Write two or three paragraphs about your book. Start each paragraph with a topic sentence using one of reasons above, then add two or three sentences giving some examples that support your reason.

Funny Books

The 6th Grade Nickname Game **Gordon Korman**	*Bunnicula* **James Howe**	*The Adventures of Ali Baba Bernstein* **Johanna Hurwitz**	*The Adventures of Captain Underpants* **Dav Pilkey**
Amber Brown (series) **Paula Danzinger**	*Stephanie's Ponytail* (picture book) **Robert Munsch**	*Chancy and the Grand Rascal* **Sid Fleischman**	*Tales of a Fourth-Grade Nothing* **Judy Blume**
Help! I'm Trapped...(series) **Todd Strasser**	*Anastasia Krupnick* (series) **Lois Lowry**	*The Great Brain* (series) **John D. Fitzgerald**	*Henry and Beezus* **Beverly Cleary**
Mr. Popper's Penguins **Richard Atwater**	*Superfudge* **Judy Blume**	*Amelia Bedelia* (series) **Peggy Parish**	*Wayside School* (series) **Louis Sacher**
The Twinkie Squad **Gordon Korman**	*The Twits* **Roald Dahl**	*Tuesday* (A wordless picture book) **David Wiesner**	*Ramona the Pest* **Beverly Cleary**
Matilda **Roald Dahl**	*Martin's Mice* **Dick King-Smith**	*Sam's Sandwich* (picture book series) **David Pelham**	*Be a Perfect Person in Just Three Days* **Stephen Manes**

Time Travel:
A Different Kind of Journey

Many of our favorite books are fantasies, and time travel is one type of fantasy. Madeleine L'Engle's *A Wrinkle in Time* is a time travel fantasy and so is Lynne Reid Banks' *Indian in the Cupboard*. In order for a book to be considered part of the time travel genre, it must contain one or more of the following motifs:

- Objects may magically transport characters from past to present or present to past.
- The setting is historically accurate.
- Details from the time period must be part of the characterization and the plot.
- Characters who have problems in the present often learn to deal with them through experiences that they have in the past.
- Characters often gain perspective from their experiences in time travel.
- There is an element of suspense as readers get a glimpse into the past or future.
- The setting and the problem are connected in some way.
- Time travelers may comment on disparities between present and past.

For this genre study, one option is to choose three or four titles that you can acquire for your classroom in sets of six or seven (paperbacks are noted) so that students in small groups can be reading different books, all with a time travel theme. Book sets can be rotated from group to group and open-ended questions used to monitor comprehension in a reading journal format. The motifs above should be discussed prior to beginning this study.

The Indian in the Cupboard
by Lynne Reid Banks
(Paperback)

The Trolley to Yesterday
by John Bellairs (Paperback)

The Children of Green Knowe
by L.M. Boston (Paperback)

The Court of the Stone Children
by Eleanor Cameron
(Paperback)

Friends in Time
by Grace Chetwin

Stonewords: A Ghost Story
by Pam Conrad (Paperback)

Reunion
by Roger Essley

Back to the Titanic
by Beatrice Gormley
(Paperback)

The Doll in the Garden:
A Ghost Story
by Mary Downing Hahn
(Paperback)

Time for Andrew
by Mary Downing Hahn
(Paperback)

A Girl Called Boy
by Belinda Hurmence
(Paperback)

The Riddle of Penncroft Farm
by Dorothea Jensen

The Secret of the Ruby Ring
by Yvonne MacGrory
(Paperback)

Culpepper's Cannon
by Gary Paulsen (Paperback)

Tom's Midnight Garden
by Philippa Pearce
(Paperback)

The Time Tree
by Enid Richemont

Knights of the Kitchen Table:
The Time Warp Trio
by Jon Scieszka (Paperback)

The Princess and the Pigpen
by Jane Resh Thomas
(Paperback)

Building Blocks
by Cynthia Voigt (Paperback)

Window of Time
by Karen Weinberg
(Paperback)

Keep the Rest of the Class Reading and Writing ... While You Teach Small Groups   Scholastic Professional Books

Name:

Time Travel: A Weekly Reading Log

Directions: You are responsible for reading one chapter each day, so you will need a new "Weekly Reading Log" sheet each week. Each day after you have read a new chapter, comment on one of the topics. You do not have to discuss them in any particular order; choose a topic that fits the chapter best. You may share ideas and work with a friend who is reading the same book.

Chapter #	Topic:	Comment:
	What are the main characters doing or learning?	
	How does the setting (where) affect the story?	
	How does the time period (when) affect the story?	
	What is suspenseful to you?	
	What problems are there? How are they being solved?	

Keep the Rest of the Class Reading and Writing ... While You Teach Small Groups Scholastic Professional Books

Happily Ever After Headlines

Directions: Newspaper headlines are written to attract attention to a story. Action verbs and short phrases tell the main idea of the story. Only a certain number of letters and spaces can be used, so words are often left out. You will be creating headlines to tell the endings of some of the fairy tales you've read. Don't tell the whole story, only how things turned out. See the example below.

Create headlines that tell the endings of these fairy tales:

STORY	HEADLINE
Puss in Boots	*Example:* **Marquis Marries Princess**
Cinderella	
Sleeping Beauty	
Snow White and the Seven Dwarfs	
Rumpelstiltskin	
Hansel and Gretel	
Tom Thumb	
Snow White and Rose Red	
Rapunzel	
The Fisherman and His Wife	
Thumbelina	
Beauty and the Beast	

Redwall: A Choice Menu

The ideas for the table below were adapted, with permission, from this excellent literature web site (http://www.carolhurst.com/titles/redwall.html). Carol Otis Hurst's comprehensive review provided the topics for a menu of choices for students reading independently or in literature study groups. She recommends this book for grades 4 and above.

Redwall
By Brian Jacques

Complete any nine activities. Check each one as it is finished.

☐ What is a fantasy? Why is this book a fantasy?	☐ Name at least five other books that are part of this series.	☐ Cluny the Scourge is the evil villain. Who is the hero? Write a paragraph about the villain and another about the hero. Describe them and your feelings about them.
☐ Each chapter begins with a pen and ink drawing that foreshadows the action. Choose one and tell about what it foreshadows. Explain its significance.	☐ Almost every chapter ends with a cliffhanger. What is a cliffhanger? Tell about a cliffhanger in this book that really made you want to keep reading.	☐ Make a list of at least six of the characters. How do their names fit their personalities?
☐ Describe some of the heroic deeds in the story.	☐ Describe some of the evil and cruel deeds in the story.	☐ Create your own map of the territories involved in the battles.
☐ The tapestry and Cluny's dream were the two major prophecies in this book. In what ways were they important? Write a paragraph about each.	☐ Both sides observed specific rules of warfare. What were some of those rules?	☐ Tell about some of the riddles and codes. How were they important to the story?

Easy Long-Term Projects

Long-term, ongoing projects maintain a work-oriented structure within the classroom. The key is that all students always have something to do. The long-term projects in this chapter are designed to last several weeks, supplementing and overlapping both centers and small-group activities. Students learn accountability and responsibility as they work toward specific goals.

Name: _____

Newbery Medal Winners and Honor Books
An Independent Study Project

Directions: You may choose one of the books listed on the next two pages or any other book that has been declared a Newbery Medal Winner or Newbery Honor Book. Your first goal is to read five of these prize-winning books. Each time you read one, complete an assignment from the list of choices below. Make sure you choose a different assignment for each book!

Assignment Choices:

☐ Summarize each chapter using complete sentences. (Minimum: three sentences)

☐ Create a crossword puzzle with one-word answers to questions about the book. (Twenty-five word minimum, use question-type clues)

☐ Write a poem about each of the important characters. (Minimum: two characters)

☐ Write a new last chapter for the book. (One page minimum)

☐ Write a three- or four-paragraph book review that includes all the story elements (setting, characters, problem, and resolution) and a final paragraph giving your opinion of the book.

☐ Write a bio-poem about the main character. (Do you have the directions?)

☐ Create a movie poster to advertise the book. (Do you have the guidelines?)

☐ Do a We/Me comparison between you and the main character

Completed by _____

Titles of Books Read:

1. _____

2. _____

3. _____

4. _____

5. _____

My favorite! _____

Keep the Rest of the Class Reading and Writing … While You Teach Small Groups   Scholastic Professional Books

Newbery Medal Winners and Honor Books
An Ongoing Independent Study Project

• *Holes* by Louis Sacher Medal Winner (1999)	• *A Long Way from Chicago* by Richard Peek Honor Book (1999)
• *Out of the Dust* by Karen Hesse Medal Winner (1998)	• *Ella Enchanted* by Gail Carson Levine Honor Book (1998)
• *Lily's Crossing* by Patricia Reilly Giff Honor Book (1998)	• *Wringer* by Jerry Spinelli Honor Book (1998)
• *The View From Saturday* by E.L. Konigsburg Medal Winner (1997)	• *Belle Prater's Boy* by Ruth White Honor Book (1997)
• *The Great Fire* by Jim Murphy Honor Book (1996)	• *The Giver* by Lois Lowry Medal Winner (1994)
• *Shiloh* by Phyllis Reynolds Naylor Medal Winner (1992)	• *The Wright Brothers: How They Invented the Airplane* by Russell Freedman Honor Book (1992)
• *Maniac Magee* by Jerry Spinelli Medal Winner (1991)	• *Number the Stars* by Lois Lowry Medal Winner (1990)
• *In The Beginning: Creation Stories from Around the World* by Virginia Hamilton Honor Book (1989)	• *Lincoln: A Photobiography* by Russell Freedman Medal Winner (1988)
• *Hatchet* by Gary Paulsen Honor Book (1988)	• *The Whipping Boy* by Sid Fleischman Medal Winner (1987)
• *Sarah, Plain and Tall* by Patricia MacLachlan Medal winner (1986)	• *Ramona Quimby, Age 8* by Beverly Cleary Honor Book (1982)
• *Bridge to Terabithia* by Katherine Paterson Medal Winner (1978)	• *Ramona and Her Father* by Beverly Cleary Honor Book (1978)

Newbery Medal Winners and Honor Books
An Ongoing Independent Study Project (page two)

- *Abel's Island*
  by William Steig
  Honor Book (1977)

- *The Grey King*
  by Susan Cooper
  Medal Winner (1976)

- *The Hundred Penny Box*
  by Sharon Bell Mathis
  Honor Book (1976)

- *M.C. Higgins, the Great*
  by Virginia Hamilton
  Medal Winner (1975)

- *Julie of the Wolves*
  by Jean Craighead George
  Medal Winner (1973)

- *Frog and Toad Together*
  by Arnold Lobel
  Honor Book (1973)

- *Mrs. Frisby and the Rats of NIMH*
  by Robert C. O'Brien
  Medal Winner (1972)

- *Annie and the Old One*
  by Miska Miles
  Honor Book (1972)

- *The Headless Cupid*
  by Zilpha Keatley Snyder
  Honor Book (1972)

- *Summer of the Swans*
  by Betsy Byars
  Medal Winner (1971)

- *Sounder*
  by William H. Armstrong
  Medal Winner (1970)

- *From the Mixed-Up Files of Mrs. Basil E. Frankweiler* by E.L. Konigsburg
  Medal Winner (1968)

- *Rascal*
  by Sterling North
  Honor Book (1964)

- *A Wrinkle in Time*
  by Madeleine L'Engle
  Medal Winner (1963)

- *Onion John*
  by Joseph Krumgold
  Medal Winner (1960)

- *My Side of the Mountain*
  by Jean Craighead George
  Honor Book (1960)

- *Old Yeller*
  by Fred Gipson
  Honor Book (1957)

- *The Courage of Sarah Noble*
  by Alice Dalgliesh
  Honor Book (1955)

- *Charlotte's Web*
  by E.B. White
  Honor Book (1953)

- *King of the Wind*
  by Marguerite Henry
  Medal Winner (1949)

Name: _____

Newbery Project: Assignment Choices

To write poems about the important characters in your book, you may use:

☐ **Two-Word Poems.** The rule is simply two words, two words, two words, two words, etc. written right down the page. Your poems should describe the character's physical characteristics and personality traits as well as the character's importance to the story. Before you put your poem together, brainstorm all the facts that impressed you about the character. Write down your ideas and then create your poem.

☐ **Telephone Poems.** Write your telephone number at the top of the page. Each number dictates the number of words that will be in each line. (Zero can be zero or 10.) Include as many facts about the character as you can.

☐ **Pyramid Poems.** There are rules for this poetry form, but for this project you may just stay with the structure. Line one, 1 word; line two, 2 words; line three, 3 words, and so on, to the eighth line with eight words, all focused on the character you are describing.

☐ **Bio-Poems:**

Use the bio-poem format to write a poem about the main character of your book.

> Line One: Character's name
>
> Line Two: Four words that describe him/her
>
> Line Three: Five words that are identifiers telling who or what he/she is
>
> Line Four: Lover of (finish this phrase by naming three things)
>
> Line Five: Who feels (finish this phrase by naming three emotions)
>
> Line Six: Who needs (finish this phrase by naming three things)
>
> Line Seven: Who gives (see above)
>
> Line Eight: Who fears (see above)
>
> Line Nine: Who likes to wear (see above)
>
> Line Ten: Who would like to see (finish this sentence)
>
> Line Eleven: Lives (give information about geographical region)
>
> Line Twelve: Repeat Line One

☐ **Movie Poster.** Imagine that the book you read is being made into a movie. It's up to you to design a poster that will make the movie a box office hit! The poster needs to have a "hook," an attention grabber that causes people to look at it and immediately want to go see the movie. Use bold lettering, quotes from the book, or quotes from people who have "seen" the movie. Use your great vocabulary and your imagination to make the movie appeal to everyone. Make it sound exciting and wonderful. (This is not a good format to use if you didn't like the book!)

☐ **We/Me Comparison.** You will need two sheets of paper to do the WE/ME Comparison between yourself and the main character. In big bubble letters on one sheet, write the word "WE." In big bubble letters on another sheet, write the word "ME." Inside the "WE," write down all the characteristics and behaviors that you share with your book's main character. Inside the "ME," write down all that differentiates you from the main character.

Name: _____

Caldecott Bingo: Five In A Row

Directions: The Caldecott Medal is presented each year to the illustrator of the most distinguished American picture book for children published in the United States. Many illustrators also write the stories that they illustrate. These books can be found in the picture book section of the library and are arranged alphabetically by the author's last name. When you have read one of these books, choose an activity on the next page.

Rapunzel by Paul O. Zelinsky	*Sam, Bangs & Moonshine* by Evaline Ness	*Black and White* by David Macaulay	*Jumanji* by Chris Van Allsburg	*One Fine Day* by Nonny Hogrogian
Abraham Lincoln by Ingri and Edgar Parin d'Aulaire	*Golem* by David Wisniewski	*Make Way for Ducklings* by Robert McClosky	*The Little House* by Virginia Lee Burton	*Smoky Night* by Eve Bunting (illustrator: David Diaz)
Arrow to the Sun: A Pueblo Indian Tale by Gerald McDermott	*Saint George and the Dragon* by Margaret Hodges (illustrator: Trina Schart Hyman)	*The Fool of the World and the Flying Ship* by Arthur Ransome (illustrator: Uri Shulevitz)	*Officer Buckle and Gloria* by Peggy Rathman	*Tuesday* by David Wiesner
The Girl Who Loved Wild Horses by Paul Goble	*The Glorious Flight* by Alice and Martin Provensen	*Grand-father's Journey* by Allen Say	*Where the Wild Things Are* by Maurice Sendak	*Many Moons* by James Thurber (illustrator: Louis Slobodkin)
The Polar Express by Chris Van Allsburg	*Fables* by Arnold Lobel	*Sylvester and the Magic Pebble* by William Steig	*Mirette on the High Wire* by Emily Arnold McCully	*Lon Po Po* by Ed Young

Keep the Rest of the Class Reading and Writing ... While You Teach Small Groups   Scholastic Professional Books

Caldecott Medal Winners: Activity Choices

Directions: From the "Caldecott Bingo: Five in a Row" chart, choose five of these award-winning picture books to read. You may read five in a row, five in a column, or five diagonally. Complete a different activity for each book, and put the book's title next to the activity. Don't forget to put an X in the square of your Bingo sheet.

Activity Choices	Book Title
Write a letter to the book's illustrator. Tell the illustrator what you liked most about the book. Tell which illustration was your favorite and why. Ask the illustrator two or three questions about the artwork in the book.	
Make up five "why" questions about the story or the illustrations. Answer the questions.	
Describe the most interesting scene in the book. Tell exactly what's in the picture and how you feel when you are looking at it.	
Create a one-page script for a play based on the story.	
What was the setting of the story? How did the illustrator help you find out about the setting? How did the setting change in the story? How did the setting help the story?	
What was the main problem of the story? How was it solved? Write a paragraph telling the problem in the first sentence and then write three more sentences that tell how it was solved.	

It's All in the Cards

Directions: Use the card catalogue or computer in your library or media center to find the Dewey Decimal Number for books about the following subjects. Write the number in the square. Read five books vertically, horizontally, or diagonally for BINGO! Complete the book report, "Create a Word Sort" or the "Alphabetical Fact Sheet."

A book about a Native American tribe	A biography	A book about your state	A book of poetry	A book about rocks and minerals
A book about sports	A book about the United States	A book about an inventor	A book about the Solar System	A book of folktales or fairytales
A book about a President	A book about an invention	FREE CHOICE	A book about basketball	A book about hobbies
A book about animals	A book about the ocean	A book about sports	An auto-biography	A book about an artist
A book about magic tricks	A book about art	A book about cats or dogs	A book about a famous person	A book about another state

Name: _____

Alphabetical Fact Sheet

Directions: Reading a nonfiction book requires attention to facts. Complete the alphabetical beginning with a sentence containing a fact from the book you've read.

A is for...	
B is for...	
C is for...	
D is for...	
E is for...	
F is for...	
G is for...	
H is for...	
I is for...	
J is for...	
K is for...	
L is for...	
M is for...	
N is for...	
O is for...	
P is for...	
Q is for...	
R is for...	
S is for...	
T is for...	
U is for...	
V is for...	
W is for...	
X is for...	
Y is for...	
Z is for...	

Name: _____ **Date:** _____

Dewey Decimal Nonfiction Book Report

Title of Book _____

Author _____

Dewey Decimal Number _____

Directions: Fill in the information above. Write a four-sentence summary of your book. Include a topic sentence, two sentences of factual information, and a closing sentence. Your closing sentence may include your opinion of the book.

_____

_____

_____

_____

_____

_____

_____

_____

_____

_____

_____

_____

_____

_____

Exploring Picture Books to Learn About Literary Devices (Set One)

Directions: Authors use words in different ways to make their writing more interesting. As you read the picture books at this center, watch for examples of these literary devices. Record the titles of the books in which you found them.

1. Alliteration: Like a tongue twister, repetition of initial sounds in two or more words

> *Example:* You'll see doves dipping down for the juicy red fruit... (From *The Desert Is Theirs* by Byrd Baylor)

2. Aphorism: Like a proverb, a concise statement expressing a general truth

> *Example:* And we don't have to make such a terrible fuss because everyone isn't exactly like us. (From *Old Henry* by Joan W. Blos)

3. Atmosphere: Using descriptions of sensory impressions to set the emotional mood and the reader's attitude

> *Example:* He could feel the pebbles on the pavement through the thin soles of his tattered shoes. (From "The Poor Old Dog" in Arnold Lobel's *Fables*)

4. Foreshadowing: A clue that the author gives that something is about to happen

> *Example:* In *The Amazing Bone*, by William Steig, the reader learns at the very beginning that the bone can imitate sounds.

5. Hyperbole: Exaggeration for effect

> *Example:* ...and for breakfast every morning he ate five dozen eggs, ten sacks of potatoes, and a half-barrel of mush made from a whole sack of cornmeal. (From "Paul Bunyan, the Mightiest Logger of Them All" by Mary Pope Osborne, in *From Sea to Shining Sea*, compiled by Amy L. Cohn)

6. Imagery: The author's sensory descriptions that create mental pictures, allowing us to imagine a scene

> *Example:* Crashing through the alder thickets beside the creeks and through the shallow creeks themselves, churning the water into a muddy foam, the mighty herd rolled on its way; and the thunder of its coming spread terror far and wide. (From *Where the Buffaloes Begin* by Olaf Baker)

Name: _____

Exploring Picture Books to Learn About Literary Devices (Set Two)

Directions: Authors use words in different ways to make their writing more interesting. As you read the picture books at this center, watch for examples of these literary devices. Record the titles of the books in which you found them.

1. Inference: **To reach a conclusion without the author actually stating it**

> *Example:* In Eve Bunting's book, *Dandelions*, you can tell that Mama is unhappy when she looks at the soddie, their new home of bricks cut from the sod, and says, "It's like a prairie dog's burrow."

2 Irony: **A combination of circumstances in which the opposite of what was expected occurs; a humorous play on words when their intended meaning is the direct opposite of their usual sense**

> *Example:* The wolf in *Hog-Eye*, by Susan Meddaugh, brings the last and most important ingredient for the soup. It is the ingredient that helps the pig escape.

3. Metaphor: **When one thing is compared to another without the use of like or as**

> *Example:* It was late in the afternoon when, at last, he sighted the lake. It lay, a gray sheet with a glint of silver, glimmering under the sun. (In Olaf Baker's *Where the Buffaloes Begin*, the lake is compared to a sheet.)

4. Parody: **When a literary work is imitated in plot or language, sometimes with humor**

> *Example:* *Somebody and the Three Blairs*, by Marilyn Tolhurst, is a parody of Goldilocks. Jon Scieszka's *The True Story of the Three Little Pigs* is a parody.

5. Personification: **When human qualities are given to an animal or an inanimate object**

> *Example:* Even the dry earth makes a sound of joy when the rain touches. (*The Desert Is Theirs* by Byrd Baylor)

6. Simile: **A comparison between two unlike things to show similarity; similes usually include the words like or as**

> *Example:* The sound of the wind in the grass was like the sound of the rivers we'd known back home. (From *Dandelions* by Eve Bunting)

Keep the Rest of the Class Reading and Writing ... While You Teach Small Groups Scholastic Professional Books

Name: _____

Literary Devices Found in Picture Books - Set One

Directions: As you locate examples of these literary devices, write the titles of the books in the appropriate spaces.

Alliteration	Aphorism	Atmosphere
Foreshadowing	**Hyperbole**	**Imagery**

Keep the Rest of the Class Reading and Writing ... While You Teach Small Groups   Scholastic Professional Books

Name: _____

Literary Devices Found in Picture Books - Set Two

Directions: As you locate examples of these literary devices, write the titles of the books in the appropriate spaces.

Metaphor	Irony	Inference
Simile	**Personification**	**Parody**

A Teacher's Guide:
Some Books to Use for Teaching Literary Devices

Alliteration	*Rotten Island* by William Steig *Zinnia* by Anita Lobel *The Desert Is Theirs* by Byrd Baylor
Aphorism	*Old Henry* by Joan Blos *Grandfather's Journey* by Allen Say
Atmosphere	*Oregon's Journey* by Rascal *The Polar Express* by Chris Van Allsburg
Foreshadowing	*Just Plain Fancy* by Patricia Polacco *Death of the Iron Horse* by Paul Goble *Hog-Eye* by Susan Meddaugh
Hyperbole	*Library Lil* by Suzanne Williams *The Best Town in the World* by Byrd Baylor
Imagery	*The Girl Who Loved Wild Horses* by Paul Goble *When I Was Young in the Mountains* by Cynthia Rylant
Inference	*Jumanji* by Chris Van Allsburg *Annie and the Old One* by Miska Miles
Irony	*Many Moons* by James Thurber *The Amazing Bone* by William Steig *The Night I Followed the Dog* by Nina Laden *Chrysanthemum* by Kevin Henkes
Metaphor	*Oregon's Journey* by Rascal *Encounter* by Jane Yolen *Where the Buffaloes Begin* by Olaf Baker
Parody	*The Paper Bag Princess* by Robert Muench *The True Story of the Three Little Pigs* by Jon Scieszka
Personification	*Sylvester and the Magic Pebble* by William Steig *The Desert Is Theirs* by Byrd Baylor *Ghost's Hour* by Eve Bunting
Simile	*Library Lil* by Suzanne Williams *The Bicycle Man* by Allen Say *The Girl Who Loved Wild Horses* by Paul Goble

As students become familiar with literary devices, add center activities such as:

- Find an example of alliteration in your reading and incorporate it into an original poem.
- Practice creating atmosphere. Write a description of a scene that will make the reader feel sympathy for someone.
- End a story with an aphorism. Find a proverb that you especially like and create a story to go with it.

Name: _____

And the Winners Are...

Directions: At the end of the school year, you will be voting for your favorites in several different categories. The categories are listed below. Use this page to keep track of your favorites during the year.

Favorite Female Character	
Favorite Male Character	
Favorite Character in a Supporting Role	
Favorite Author	
Favorite Animal (in an animal story)	
Favorite Illustrator	
Favorite Picture Book	
Favorite Chapter Book	
Favorite Readaloud	
Favorite Poet	
Funniest Author	
Favorite Newbery Prize Winner	
Favorite Caldecott Winner	